Gay Brewer chipping to the green at St. Andrews.

SBN 361 01517 8
© 1970 Bagenal Harvey Organisation
Published in 1970 by Purnell, London, W.1
Made and printed in Great Britain
by Purnell & Sons Ltd., Paulton (Somerset) and London

The World of
Golf

18/-
90 n.p.

Mike Bonallack explodes

THE WORLD OF
GOLF

Reporters
E. R. "TED" DEXTER
and
MICHAEL McDONNELL

PURNELL,
London, W.1.

CONTENTS

The publishers wish to thank the following for per-
mission to reproduce drawings, cartoons and photo-
graphs:
Frank Gardner
Haymarket Press
Mansell Collection
Punch
Syndication International
The Sport and General Press Agency

Michael McDonnell is the *Daily Mail* golf correspondent

INTRODUCTION by E. R. "TED" DEXTER

Tell me another one, just like the other one — tell me another one do. This old music hall favourite tells us something about human nature: about our need to be told a story now and again, even if it's a story heard before.

It is also true that some of the oldest jokes in the world get the biggest laughs, but only if they are brought up to date and given a contemporary setting.

An Annual of this kind only exists because of the human need which demands it and can only satisfy its readers if the old joker, the game of golf itself, is portrayed in his newest set of clothes.

So that is what we have set out to do here: to cover as carefully as we can the fantastically broad field of sporting entertainment which golf now provides for the world, with an obvious emphasis on the great professionals who play the game best but with an occasional sidestep off the fairway into the rough and hazards of the club golfers' weekend exploits.

If the reader happens to be Jack Nicklaus passing a restful hour between tournaments then we think he will recognise a fair assessment of the world he so often dominates and illuminates with his superlative play.

If, on the other hand, you are making first acquaintance with the remarkable world of golf, we hope that this first encounter turns out to be a pleasant one and forms the beginning of a long and enduring friendship.

GOLF COURSES OLD AND NEW

You can never please everyone. This is the first lesson a golf architect learns when he starts the intricate and laborious business of turning virgin land into a golf course. There is no blueprint, no accepted authority on just how eighteen holes should look or even on how they should play, which, if nothing else, means that the man responsible for designing our adult playgrounds has the same heady but daunting freedom of choice as the writer before he starts to fill clean sheets of paper.

It is an unusual mixture of golfer, engineer and man of the soil who can successfully landscape and manicure the necessary two hundred acres until it becomes worthwhile golfing country. He must be a modern Capability Brown, the man who fashioned so many of the country house parklands and managed to leave them looking more natural than nature itself.

Just to give an idea of the engineering problems I hope I can relate the circumstances surrounding the still incomplete earth workings at the fifteenth hole on the New Course at Sunningdale: relate them, that is, without hurting people's feelings, because when one committee member's plan for adding a simple water hazard—just a bulldozer for a day and some grass seed—remains a muddy, murky apology for a puddle for a period of years, then obviously there are bound to be those who feel sensitive.

Sometimes the simplest looking things turn out to be the most complicated, or, if not complicated, in need of some special knack or insight which only comes from long practice and experience. If this is true of magicians and Cordon Bleu cooks it also applies, and more so, to the man who thinks he can make water stay the size and depth he wants, flow in the right direction and generally behave in such a way that the surrounding area is not turned overnight into swampland.

11

No names, no pack drill, so the erstwhile Walker Cup golfer who brought the dream of glinting blue water from its natural home in America to his native Berkshire heathland shall remain anonymous. His credentials as a golfer, thinker and professional man are, to say the least, extremely sound and it is hardly fair to expect to find the further attributes of the landscape gardener all bound up in the same man. It simply makes the point to say that the present state of this ill-fated water hazard, now in its fifth year and the recipient of fairly constant attention throughout the time, would give a visitor reasonable grounds for thinking it the fresh result of "just a bulldozer for a day and some grass seed". As a functional trap for the nervous slice it just about serves its purpose, but it will be some time yet before the colour magazines can use a photograph of it in their glamour section.

Of course, the very idea that golf courses should look attractive to the eye is comparatively new. St. Andrews never earned a certificate in that department either for the course itself, which, if photographed from about twenty feet looking across its surface, resembles nothing if not a lunar landing ground. Carnoustie was never intended to be easy on anything, least of all easy on the eye, and we must also remember the mass of purely functional urban golf courses, straight up and down between the houses with only a prize marrow in an adjoining allotment claiming a second glance.

I suppose the jet-age and Madison Avenue have combined to make lush green fairways, whiter than white bunkers, and palm trees against the sky line the unique selling features of golf courses all over the world.

Ally those Technicolor elements to a grand natural setting and you have the perfect product for the high speed, long distance travelling man of today.

Occasionally, where the available ingredients fall too far short of the norm, a concession is made to circumstance, to local colour and to the quaint customs of the natives.

Allan Brown, styled as a U.S.G.A. official, writes pleasingly of his personal enjoyment of the bizarre in a Pan-Am Guide to Golf Courses round the world.

Gene Sarazen, in the same publication, goes to the trouble of wearing a Tyrolean jerkin to suit the mood of playing in the Swiss Alps, but, by and large, it is not too hard to induce the camera's eye to make Bermuda look like Belgium, look like Berkshire, look like Banff, Alberta.

I reproduce a snippet from the introduction to this Golf Course Guide:— "The black sand (greens) of Ndola; the caddie house made of cornstalks at Kilembe Mines: the green located in the middle of an ancient race track in Goma: the termite proof concrete tees at the Mombasa Golf Club: the hexagonal clubhouse at Mnazi Mnoza Sports Club in Zanzibar; the shadows of the great pyramids near the 18th green at Cairo's Mena House Golf Course..."

I can add oddities myself, like the blind short hole, the 7th at the Menaggio and Cadenabbia Golf Club above Lake Como, Italy, which measured only sixty

Wentworth, 7th Green, West Course.

13

eight metres from the very back tee: a hole which needed real nerve to hit through with the most lofted club available and then a working knowledge of the local lingo to know that "buono per un due" meant that you were putting for a two.

"Lunga" was self-explanatory and meant a well nigh impossible pitch back over a vertical bank.

These eccentricities in golf provide a bit of fun but more and more, we are expected to feel at ease only in the super surroundings of the latest American golfing dream world.

Never again can I take the same homely pride in our British showpieces, Gleneagles, Turnberry, Wentworth, Birkdale and their many counterparts; not since a visit to Florida, where a five-star hotel is likely to have the same number of golf courses for its guests to play on. The Doval Golf and Country Club, Miami, is just one such mammoth complex, a golfing holiday resort quite beyond anything we know in our little islands. If you put Muirfield, Carnoustie and a couple of Lancashire coastal links all together in one place and imagine the Savoy Hotel as the clubhouse then you have some idea of the scale of this enterprise, catering to the great North American and Canadian golfing migration to the winter sunshine of Florida.

The days are fast going, I'm afraid, when a golf course can be an accident of nature where a few keen clubmen combine to mow the greens and enjoy the ageless fun of chasing that little ball round their own meadow. They will be lured away to the world of pop-up watering systems and electric caddy cars by the call of the advertising man in much the same way as many budding musicians have been lured from their instruments by the long playing record.

Golf has come of age in this respect so that every new course built has man-made, fully intended problems and hazards with very little left to chance.

People complain that the new deal lacks the charm of the old, where the courses were tailored to fit the ground rather than the other way round. There is much to be said for their point of view, but there is also much to learn from the modern courses which have gone a long way towards satisfying all golfers, whether low handicap, high handicap, professional or beginner. For instance, it has taken all too long to appreciate the simplicity of the single long teeing ground, sometimes a hundred yards in length. For one thing maintenance is made easy and then there is the personal choice of playing the white (forward), red (middle) or blue (back) markers. To see the system working is to accept how much better it is than having half-a-dozen tees, none of them big enough, dotted around at various angles to the green. In this scheme of things you often find that the very back tee or tiger tee is the only one which is properly placed in relation to the hazards and yet this tee gets to be used only a couple of times per year. The new system presents every golfer with exactly the same problem according to his ability, and everyone is entitled to bite off just as

Royal Birkdale.

15

much of the golf course as he thinks he can chew.

Another common criticism of the newly-designed courses is the lack of rough; no carries from the tee, no heather, no gorse, nor, in some cases, any trees.

My way of changing their minds would be to lead them gently onto the East course of the U.S.P.G.A. National, Palm Beach Gardens, Florida, and then invite them to estimate their chances of playing within four strokes of their handicap. All they have to do is to negotiate a golf lay-out which owes nothing to the long gone days of the wooden shaft and guttie balls. Every bunker, slope and water-hazard, each single green, its approaches and surrounds, has been designed to test modern golfers with modern equipment. The highest point on the course is not more than twenty feet above sea level so there are no excuses accepted for tired legs or tales of exaggerated up-hill down-hill and side-hill stances. The locals will happily challenge a scratch amateur golfer to break eighty the first few times round.

With hardly a tree to be seen and no rough to speak of you may wonder what can possibly make golf so difficult and it was a question I had to ask myself after battling round three times with scant success.

Its hidden menace lay mainly in never giving you a second chance—or, to be more colloquial—it never gives a sucker an even break. If you drive the wrong side of the fairway, let alone getting snarled up with bunkers and acres of water, then you can already wave good-bye to any chance of a birdie. That golf course just picks off your mistakes one by one until just half-a-dozen semi-errors leave you fighting an up-hill contest against the dreaded eighties.

You will be playing the big-ball, remember, on wiry fairways which give little run, where a four hundred yard hole is just never reduced to a drive and a flick—unless of course you happen to be Jack Nicklaus with a gale of wind at your back. It is a very different story from, for instance, the eighteenth at St. Andrews, three hundred and fifty eight yards, which Nicklaus contrived to actually drive, four times out of four in the British Open.

Before I go overboard about one particular course or type, I must register a criticism of my own which concerns a good many "architect designed" putting greens. There seems to be a vogue for raising the surface to exactly eye level with a gentle sloping approach through a narrow bunkered opening and steeper banks falling away to the sides and rear. Better drainage is one result and a terror of missing the green another. These are not the problems. My quarrel is over the matter of judging distance to these eye-level pins where the greens are sometimes forty yards from front to back. In practice it is possible to play a goodish shot, having selected a club on a trial and error basis, and still be no wiser about whether the ball lies short or past the pin even though the white dot is clearly visible on the green: How one is supposed to judge distance accurately before playing I'm damned if I know.

16

The famous "Postage Stamp" hole at Troon, Scotland.

WG – B

The only way seems to be to go through the whole process of measurement from a particular fairway spot to the centre of the green and then to walk forward on the day, or send your caddie to check the placing of the hole. That is all very well for tournament play but in general it can only be one more factor contributing towards slow play, and anything that does that should be subjected to very close scrutiny before being accepted as in the best interests of golf.

So what constitutes the perfect course to play on? It is a question which, in the context of other games, barely invites argument.

Snooker tables may vary marginally but at least they are intended to be identical. The same goes for tennis courts, squash courts, and even cricket pitches. Golf, on the other hand, has nothing in its rules to say how long or short a course should be, how wide the fairway or how deep a bunker. There is no way of regulating the wind or the rain or just how much the grass should grow in any one day. It means that every time you play round even the same course, there is always a new ticklish assignment to be faced, with the only absolute certainty being the size of the hole you are trying to reach.

Making up a composite course from the very best holes you have ever encountered is probably the only way each person can satisfy his or her own ideals.

Mine would include the short 5th hole at Royal Worlington near Newmarket and the razor edge 4th at Rye, Sussex. The trouble is that acknowledged great holes, like the 7th at Pebble Beach, are all so damnably difficult that we would never get round.

So we must temper our ideal assortment of holes with a touch of humanity, place them in a setting where there is at least something better than vegetable marrows to catch our attention, just to pass the time of day when concentration on golf momentarily fails, and then go play there in our imagination every time we have a chance to daydream.

St. Andrews—aerial view of part of the "Loop".

CATHERINE THE GREAT

PEDIGREE in human sport has rarely counted for much. Indeed, the offspring of the famous can find their family tradition too much of a handicap to follow the same path.

Catherine Lacoste is the incredible exception. At the age of 24, this French woman has retired from serious competition simply because there are no more worlds to conquer and she sees no value in tournament golf for its own sake. Not only that, but she had done enough in a six-year career to escape the shadow of her famous parents. Her father, Rene Lacoste, was three-times Wimbledon tennis champion, and her mother, Simone de la Chaume, was French gold champion six times and took the British title once.

Catherine undoubtedly inherited an athletic talent, but much more valuable was an inbred competitive streak she was never able to forget. She recalls that her grandfather once told her: "Whatever you choose, tennis or golf, you must be the best."

In 1967 she breezed into the tough American women's circuit and, against all the odds, became Open champion. In 1969, she completed her Grand Slam. She won the French Closed and Open titles, the British championship, and then endured the blistering heat of Texas to earn the American amateur title. After which, she decided to stop.

"I am honestly fed up with all the pressure," she confessed at the time. "I get to a tournament and feel I don't want to play. If you win people say it's normal and if you don't they say you're slipping. It's hard to play in a tournament like that.

"Golf is a tough game. You have to hang on when it's all going badly. You've got to keep yourself under control even though you may feel temperamental inside. I've learned to be tough on the outside. But each time you win, you lose a little of your sensitivity. And that is a bad thing for a girl."

She has not always been popular with her contemporaries, and not simply because of the exceptional talent which she seems to turn on in a casual

Right: The aggression of a champion—even in trouble, Catherine Lacoste still hits the ball hard from a bunker—and keeps her head down after impact. After all, she knows where the ball is going!

manner. She has a cruel frankness which to her is honesty but to others sounds like brashness.

She says: "I have an open nature and have always believed in saying what I feel. But not in the way it always sounded. I don't think I've ever said anything nasty, consciously."

If the tigresses of the American professional tour expected deference during the 1967 Open championship, they were to be disappointed. Catherine has that clear-eyed confidence that is rooted possibly in the formidable affluence of her family. Her parents own the golf course in the South of France where she learned to play. They have a home there, plus another in the country and an apartment in Paris. Such a background is never likely to breed self-doubt.

None of the top women players were disposed to treat her very kindly during practice rounds and it reflected badly on them. Yet she was to have her revenge, if she ever saw it as such. While these tournament-hardened players tackled the course in Hot Springs, Virginia, with excessive caution, Catherine ripped into it. After two rounds, she was five strokes clear and even opened that margin to seven strokes in the final round. But she was fallible enough to throw six of them away in a spasm of nervous errors. She retrieved an iron grip on herself to birdie the seventeenth hole and become Open champion by two strokes. The professionals took the money, but Catherine had dealt them a mortal blow. She had the title.

Only in her last season did she win the British title and explained: "I had been playing since I was 18 and it made me really mad that I couldn't win. I wanted it, among other things, for sentimental reasons."

She recovered resolutely in the final against Ann Irvin, after being three down, and won by a hole. Some said she was lucky because earlier a crucial shot struck a spectator, bounced on to the green and saved her from trailing even further behind. But it is the mark of a champion that whatever the break, good or bad, it is accepted with the same, almost fatalistic, grace. And Catherine produced brilliant golf after the episode to wear down Ann Irvin and earn the title.

Later that year, she went to Texas. She meant to win the American title. And it proved to be a classic example of her skill, stamina and courage. Despite the fierce Texas sun which forced her to shelter under an umbrella between every shot and wear a damp towel around her neck, she stayed close to par golf for six rounds. It was enough to complete her Slam.

Her technique is impressive. She has a man's power and can thrash a drive 250 yards and despatch a one-iron around 200 yards. For such a small person, she has a surprisingly full and upright swing. But her main fault comes from an eagerness to lash the ball which sometimes causes her to hit too early.

Her greatest quality, and the one which must have irritated her more solemn-minded rivals, is an ability to treat the whole thing as great fun yet bring to it

22

a formidable competitive drive. She is as happy playing golf with friends as she is in major tournaments.

"I am one of those French women who likes to spend all day in Oxford Street just looking at the clothes," she says. "I could never have been a professional because that kind of life is too tough and perhaps too serious for me."

Her attitude is such that she will not be tempted to try again for the Grand Slam of women's golf. She is already preparing for her new role as a housewife — with cookery lessons. Yet her father remains convinced that she could become a world-class tennis player. But she just smiles: "I couldn't go through all THAT again."

The best woman amateur golfer in the world can still have doubts about a putt. Here Lacoste takes advice from Beverley Huke.

"THE BLACK KNIGHT"

GARY PLAYER has an ambition to quit World golf by the time he is forty. Not that he will. But the thought makes the present 100,000-miles-a-year pilgrimage a little easier to bear.

He is a millionaire who can never live like one. For him, the routine is just another aeroplane, another hotel and another golf course. You don't have to be a millionaire to live like that.

"The only time I realise I'm wealthy is when I go home to my farm in South Africa," he says. "I can look out and, for as far as I can see, I can say that it belongs to me. For the rest of the time, I feel no different now than when I first came to Britain as a raw kid and shared a room at ten bob a night."

His is probably the greatest golf talent in the world because nobody can adapt to various conditions as quickly or as consistently as this South African. He moves into peak efficiency as soon as the bell goes. His golf swing has been carefully fashioned to work anywhere in the world and he has an ox-like constitution which withstands the time differentials of jet travel and the vagaries of diet wherever he plays.

On top of all this, he is an inspirational player who draws heavily on the belief that there is some divine purpose behind his golf career. Billy Casper, who combines evangelistic work with his golf, once cracked: "God must certainly have a problem now. People say I think He's on my side. But Gary Player says He's on his. How can we both win tournaments?"

But Player says: "I don't actually pray for victory at golf because all the other guys might be praying too. But I sometimes feel that the guy upstairs has got everything planned. And if it isn't your turn, well that's the way it's got to be."

He is one of the few men to have won all four major golf titles in the world—

Right: Henry Cotton warned Player he would never stay at the top of big-time golf unless he built up his physique. The South African's tree-trunk arms show how well he learned the lesson!

24

25

and he started his second Slam by winning the 1968 British Open again.

The circumstances of some wins caused critics, somewhat unfairly, to label him as a lucky player. He won the U.S. Masters because Arnold Palmer took six on the last hole. His first British Open at Muirfield in 1959 should have been lost. He took six on the last hole himself then broke down and cried because he thought he'd thrown it away. But so did everybody else.

Player's retort to all this is simple: "The more I practise the luckier I get. Once when I was going to Pretoria, I sat on the plane with my arms folded because I didn't want anybody to see my hands. They were red raw. I'd practised until they bled. I'd been hitting golf shots for eight hours a day. I wouldn't leave a bunker until I'd holed a few shots. I didn't do all that just to be lucky. I've worked for it."

He endures a love-hate relationship with big time golf. Like Arnold Palmer and Jack Nicklaus, he became a millionaire and heads a vast international industry. Yet the more successful he becomes, the less time he can give to things which he considers important.

He is a devoted family man with five children and runs up enormous tele-

The famous Player punch—used only when the ball drops into the hole and since copied by thousands of golfers all over the world.

And the one that got away: even a champion can't hole them all. But it didn't matter — the South African was just about to win the British Open for the second time.

phone bills with daily chats to them from wherever he happens to be in the world.

"Just before I left home some time ago," he says, "I was walking with my son. He looked up at the sky and said he hoped it would rain tomorrow so I couldn't go away. It broke me up. How can you ever put a price on that sort of sacrifice?

"Yet being the best demands a total commitment. There's no other way. That's why I have this dream to be back farming by the time I'm forty. I want to be the best golfer in the world and that means giving everything. But it's a high price to pay."

INSTRUCTION

by Ted Dexter

TAKEN as a group, professional golfers are probably as amiable and honest a bunch of men as you would be likely to find: except, that is, in the matter of teaching others to play the game. It is almost as though they conspire amongst themselves to restrict all worthwhile knowledge to their own inner circle.

They write about the swing, photograph it, broadcast about it and give innumerable hints to anyone prepared to listen, but the subtlety of their scheme for keeping the amateur in his place is fairly obvious: to anyone, that is, who has tried to fight his way through the labyrinth of conflicting roads to success offered by the friendly professional.

The first giveaway comes when you actually take a live lesson. "Well, now, let's see you hit one, shall we?" starts the apparently well-intentioned tutor. "Oh, dear. Never mind. Try another one and watch the ball this time."

After a few hits and misses, he takes the club to show where you went wrong and kindly spells out exactly how it should be done. The action is described in detail, and shown to you graphically with a couple of perfect shots made with a rhythmic swing and full follow-through. You carry this image of perfection with you, suffering agonies when your attempts to copy it fall so far short of the ideal.

In despair your game deteriorates, as, even on the good days when you achieve that high finish, your head is so full of swing imagery that the putts never drop and your score remains, as ever, high in the eighties or nineties.

Then, one day, you happen to be watching a tournament and you chance upon the teacher who was responsible for all your feelings of inadequacy: the very source of your frustration and inhibition.

Out of deference to a Superior Being you tag along for a couple of holes expecting to see the same miracle of relaxed timing and precision. But no.

Your professional is now playing for money, amongst his own kind, and is no longer in the business of selling sweet swings to the gullible and greedy. He no longer stands balanced and statuesque at the finish of his drive but flails himself off his feet and dances a tune to persuade the ball away from the line of bunkers.

His second shot with an iron is hit a short flat ugly blow with hands twisted over and round the body, but the ball still finds its way to the edge of the green. Two sharp raps with the putter and your god has made his par four; and his pupil has made a discovery: Golf is to do with shifting the ball from tee to green in the way that best suits. All that technical stuff is kept for the sales-room while the real business gets done on the factory floor.

It's the same story in the books. Page 71, Lesson 3 in Ben Hogan's *Modern Fundamentals of Golf* tells us that "when you finish your backswing, your chin should be hitting against the top of your left shoulder . . . my golf shirts have a worn down spot at this particular spot."

Just imagine all the unfortunates who now spend their time hitting their chins against the top of their left shoulders instead of hitting the club head against the back of the ball. And this is only one case of getting us to think about everything but the job in hand.

In one book alone, *Tips from the Top*, I am invited to:

"grip the club as if holding a small bird";

"take a towel, tie a knot in it and stick the knot under the right armpit"; and, when putting, "to throw the right palm into the hole".

As if these proposals are not enough to turn me into a right-handed bird catcher with a painful armpit — I read further of the merits of that apparent pause at the top of the good golf swing. The book explains that the average golfer who wants to get the feeling of this so-called pause can do so if he times his swing by saying to himself, "Swing back and through": the "and" taking care of the moment in which the wrists reverse into the downswing.

I rushed away to practise, with good initial results and then the progressive deterioration inevitably followed. I returned to the book to see if I had missed anything to account for my lack of success and, of course, I had indeed been over-eager, and I had failed to read the punch line. "What makes for the pausing effect," the sermon concluded, "is leaving out all effort to achieve it."

There you are, you see. It's what I have been saying all along. The professionals don't mind in the least discussing the game with you, but sooner or later you get to realise that what you don't already have, you never can get. Not from them anyway.

The student in search of improving his game has other sources not mentioned so far. He can follow the pin-men depicted by the anonymous Mr X in the

golf magazines, or delve even deeper into the mechanics of what he tries to do in an authoritarian work such as *The Search for the Perfect Swing*. Here he can immerse himself in a whole new world of hub action, planes, pronation, hinging, supinating momentum, rotation, arching and cocking.

He can learn with amazement that even his own laboured action will cause the ball to experience air-flow wake, eddies, spin, lift and drag, though the only foreseeable purpose in assimilating this kind of information is to use it discreetly to the detriment of his club opponents.

Beware the written word. Treat every new explanation of the American method, square method, English style or any other style with the suspicion it deserves, and you may be nearer to keeping intact what little skill you possess.

If all those who look for the "secret" of golf in books and films and exhibitions, spent the same amount of time in intelligent practice there is little doubt that their scores would improve dramatically, and if human beings were not both garrulous and lazy they would do just that. But the temptation is too great. To cut the corners and get there the easy way on a potted instructional diet is so much more convenient and, in its own way, entertaining.

We love our cosy professional for his perpetual promise to lower our handicap with just a few lessons. He seems to believe in us and we want to believe in him. He really is such a nice man.

Cricket Cavalier Ted Dexter (left) practising what the pros Max Faulkner (right) and Ben Hogan preach.

PALMER'S LAST DAYS

ARNOLD PALMER, according to the theory, is his own worst enemy. The furious style which made him a legend is self-destructive. No man, not even Palmer, can maintain that sort of pace.

His golf swing has a punishing ferocity. His brazen aggression drains him mentally. And his business empire is not only a distraction but deadens any compulsion to win at all costs. The theory can be dismissed by the simple fact that, since 1957, Palmer has not dipped out of America's top ten money-winners. Nevertheless, it holds a grain of truth.

Palmer set his own standards and has always been judged against them. His success is measured in terms of championships—the British Open, the American Open and the American Masters. But for six years of the last decade, he was without a title of any consequence.

Not that this blunted the Palmer magic. As an American folk hero, his appeal was constant. A hundred people would stand around just to watch him take his clubs from the boot of his car. They would rather watch *him* play badly than anybody else play well. Palmer brought drama and excitement even to a bad score.

But the theory about his decline gained strength during the worst period of Palmer's career when, for eighteen months, he did not win a tournament on his native soil. It hardened into a conviction that he was finished. All the signs were there. Perhaps it had started as far back as 1966 when his supreme confidence was shattered by the loss of a seven-stroke lead with only nine holes of the American Open remaining. He threw away the title.

But in 1969 his ordeal reached a new intensity. He was forced to prove he

32

Palmer on himself: "I've never had much trouble hitting the ball on the fairway to the green. But even when I'm winning now the old familiar touch with the putter is not quite there. But I know it will come back. It's nothing to do with getting old."

33

G—C

was good enough to even play in the American Open. He had to take his chance in a qualifying round with a hundred other "scrubbers". But he got his place. Then came the ultimate capitulation. He walked out of the American PGA championship at Dayton, Ohio, after a first round 82 which was the worst score of his professional career.

He blamed his weakened left hip and, before boarding his £700,000 personal jet, said: "I've always played with a strong left side. It's part of my game. But I can't play like this. I will not play again until this has cleared up. No matter how long it takes."

Of course, they said, it COULD be his hip. But it might be his age. He was nearly forty and still trying to play with the furious style of a younger man. The newspapers sensed something more serious. They proclaimed: "The end of the Palmer Era"; "The King is Dead"; "He can't play like Arnold Palmer any more." One magazine was even moved to print a black-edged cover with the simple words: "Arnold Palmer R.I.P." printed thereon.

The head-down confidence of a man who knows he can get out of trouble. Palmer follows the old rule: "Don't look up too soon. You might not like what you see."

If nothing else, all the fuss reflected the essential appeal of Palmer. He was the penniless pro, who eloped with a rich man's daughter, lived in a caravan, then made his own millions. It was all the more sad because Palmer still wanted desperately to play golf. He enjoyed and distrusted his wealth. Despite his fortune, he was reluctant to leave Latrobe, his childhood town, or even the house which he and his wife bought with his first winnings. As the money rolled in, he built extra rooms for his family and offices for his personal staff. But the old homestead remained. Palmer wanted the professional tour, the only life he knew.

With only two weeks of the 1969 American circuit left, he went down to South Carolina for the Heritage Classic. It was not an important event and only three of the top ten money-winners had bothered to turn up. Palmer was then 29th in the money list. Suddenly it all came back, the glories, the disasters, the old Palmer fire. He was about to write a postscript on the decade he had influenced. Nobody begrudged him that honour. A handful of professionals clustered round the last green as Palmer, the tournament almost won, came up the fairway. None of them wanted any other conclusion.

One of the pros, Bert Yancy, echoed their sentiment as he stood in the crowd and, in a whisper, said: "Just play it safe, man. Just put it on the middle of the green." Palmer obliged and the drought was over.

"I think this is one of my most important wins," he said afterwards. "I wanted to win this tournament as much as the Open or the Masters. I felt more anxiety than I have in a long time."

That, in itself, should have been enough to silence the critics. But Palmer was not finished with them. He flew home to Latrobe, went on to New York for business, then came back to Florida a day later for the Danny Thomas-Diplomat Classic—the last tournament of the decade.

He was six strokes behind Gay Brewer, the leader, as they went into the final round. If ever there was a moment designed for a legendary Palmer charge—this was it. And Fate granted him one more favour. He ripped into the course and took only 33 strokes to reduce the front nine holes to ashes. Brewer was only one stroke ahead. Palmer devoured even that and came to the last green. His ball was twenty feet from the hole and needed to drop to make him the winner. It scampered across the grass like a frightened mouse and disappeared into the hole. Palmer had done it again.

"Getting it going again is probably the thing I wanted most in my life," he confessed. "I knew it was going to happen, that I would play again. But I didn't know when."

He had earned over £18,000 in two weeks and moved once again into America's top ten money-winners. Perhaps he would never dominate again in the classic Palmer tradition. But he had proved that, like the sleeping tiger, he could be formidable still when roused.

35

GRASS WIDOWS

"Well, it doesn't overawe me!"

"It's such a relief—I spent all morning pushing a trolley round Jay's Supermarket."

"Hurry up. Other people are waiting to use the bunker."

THE AMERICAN CIRCUIT
TOWNSEND – HOW LONG WILL IT TAKE?

IT WAS a cold blustery morning in March with the wind blowing in our faces on the first hole of the New Course at Sunningdale: typical conditions for the first round of the Sunningdale Foursomes, which provide such a useful warm-up for the golfing summer season.

I was playing with the home professional Arthur Lees, never anything but an interesting and entertaining exercise, and it would be true to say that neither of us had the slightest idea who we were playing against. One opponent looked old and the other young enough to be his grandson and that's about as much as we cared. Golf is a game with enough worries of its own without fussing too much about the opposition.

Anyway, the elder of the two played the tee shot, a respectable one, if on the short side, which reached less than half way up the first uphill incline of the fairway. As I said, it was cold, and old bones are entitled to take time to warm up.

Then the young man stepped up, whipped a brassie out of the bag and took a slashing practice swing which encouraged us to think that it would result more often in length than direction: then without a second's hesitation he hammered that ball out and beyond the brow of the hill, boring on through the wind, slap bang into the heart of the green.

I forget which year it was exactly in the early sixties but the name of the brown-eyed fresh-faced little bundle of golfing energy and ability was not to be forgotten so easily. Peter Townsend was not going to allow us to forget him from that very moment, with a string of Amateur tournament victories in the next couple of years.

The sixties were indeed golden years for Townsend. But now, change the scene to Miami, Florida, February 1970, and the second round of the $150,000 Doval-Eastern Tournament.

Making his way slowly, steadily, up the eighteenth fairway you recognise the same small, but now more stocky figure, which is unmistakably Townsend. The practice swing is more studied and the second shot played solidly for the safe side of the green. The face has less mobility, like the swing, though nothing has changed the essential underlying good humour.

37

Peter Townsend is the young man most likely to succeed. But, like Ben Hogan, his success may be a gradual thing.

With two well struck putts, he registers his par four, for a 75, which added to his first round 73 and almost certainly means that he will not make the cut for the final two rounds.

It is a very different story from amateur days when, in tough conditions like those at Doval, that score could easily have been a winning one. There is an element of relief in failing to qualify for the final two rounds, even though a

38

player may feel he has it in him to shoot a couple of real par-busters and so get in the money.

He can make a good start in his own time on the journey to the next tournament. He has time to reflect on his disappointment, to practise, to readjust his attitude, to sharpen his concentration in time for the obligatory Tuesday qualifying of the next event. But it still cannot eradicate the feeling of failure. Just to qualify a man needs every bit of skill and luck he can lay his hands on, as I learned when I tried to do just that at Doval.

They ran a special pre-qualifying event on the Friday, the week before the tournament for which they received an entry of some sixty-one professional golfers and three amateurs, of which I was one. The professionals were a mixed bunch of club pros and driving range pros who were not in possession of the player's ticket which lets them in direct to the main qualifying stage.

Nevertheless, the odd name among them rang a bell and it was confirmed to me later that some of them had indeed been regular tournament players, making their living that way, only a couple of years before. I was starting to realise the problems which face a new-boy trying to make a start in this fiercely competitive business.

These sixty golfers were playing for just nine places, not, I stress, nine places in the tournament, but the top nine players to go forward and join two hundred Tournament Player Division ticket-holding professionals in the Tuesday qualifier.

The course we played was "tougher than hell", as they say over there, the greens unfortunately underprepared and the pins placed in the most screwball awkward places I ever saw. Not that it mattered. It was the same for everybody and my seventy-three was the best score and those on seventy-six also won their slender Tuesday chance.

I was kicking myself in a way, as one so often does after a medal round. There were two short putts missed and then a foolish attempt to cut too big a slice off one of the angled water hazards cost another shot or two. I was disappointed because, once over the first hurdle, I felt that I might find some extra confidence and go further. It was not till later that I realised to what extent I had been kidding myself.

I had fondly imagined that the two hundred Tuesday qualifiers would be shooting for a substantial number of places amongst the regular 144 who set out on the Thursday, so it really knocked the wind out of my sails when it transpired that there were only nine places still open: all the other 135 places were already filled by the various exemptions.

So, of an original two hundred and sixty-four scratch or nearly scratch golfers, two hundred and fifty-five of them were to go straight home again — not just empty handed, but with never a chance of dipping their hand in the pot. It was almost comforting to know that none of the nine survivors from the

Moody: the ex-army sergeant, part-Red Indian, who chose the 1969 U.S. Open as his first win in professional golf. He putts cross-handed, right hand below the left. A solemn man among American touring professionals, he is a founder of a Bible-study Group.

Peter Townsend found his old aggression when he played a vital role in Britain's historic Ryder Cup effort against the United States at Royal Birkdale in 1969. His problem is to keep that confidence when he is playing for himself.

first qualifying stage remained in contention after the second.

In the face of this eye-opener I had to reassess all my preconceived notions about what it takes for a foreign pro to make anything like a success out of a raid on the American circuit.

I had to even rethink the basic question asked in the title of this chapter: "How long will it take Townsend?"

How long will it take him to do what? To become a top-class professional golfer? No. He is that already and has proved it many times over. What then? To measure up to Tony Jacklin? That may be more to the point and so one reminds oneself of exactly what Jacklin has done in America. The truth is that he won only one solitary tournament, at Jacksonville, in four years of constant endeavour. That he came back in good form and with the experience to win the British Open was a bonus and perhaps slightly beside the point. He went on to take the great opportunity of winning the 1970 American Open in his stride because he had already proved to himself that, on his day, he was a match for any one of four hundred regular tournament players on the American circuit, a state of mind which only comes when you actually beat the Americans, clear and cold, on their own ground.

This then is what will make or break Townsend. Who had ever heard of Orville Moody till he won his Open? Yet I met a friend of his in the States who swore vehemently that he is now and has been for some years, the finest striker of the ball out of the lot of them.

It was only *after* Lee Trevino had won his Open that people started to speak reverently of the way he stays down long and low after hitting the ball.

If good striking and general golfing ability were the only prerequisites we would have expected to hear of these great golfers before, as well as after, it happened to be their turn to win.

In much the same way, a whole host of insular Americans will never give Townsend a thought until he takes them by surprise with the couple of inspired low rounds and that last round hang-on which is the usual pattern for getting your nose in front. Only then will they start to talk of Townsend's Hogan-like swing and striking action, of his cheerful good humour and his boyish English looks.

I suppose I have begged the question "Can he win an American tournament?" and my answer is unequivocal. I am quite sure he can and will though it might take him, like many other fine players, nearly a lifetime to achieve. If that is his total committed objective, then he will surely justify my faith in him.

The only problem is working out a philosophy which sets aside the disappointments and which can accept the fact that this golf circuit is probably the toughest sporting arena yet devised and no one need be ashamed or think a jot less of themselves if their turn to win never comes.

41

EMOTION

Gary Player wipes away the tears. He stands on Carnoustie's last green—Open champion for the second time.

Right: Bembridge: The quiet moment in a round when a man asks himself, "Is it all worth it?" Maurice learned the answer later: British Matchplay Champion, Ryder Cup and an £8,000-a-year income!

Max Faulkner: the "Clown Prince of Golf", lets the mask slip as he wonders about the fate of a drive.

Tony Horton shows anguish at a missed putt. .

Even Billy Casper, the best putter in the world, still gets delighted when a long one drops.

"SUPER MEX"

HE wears a sticking plaster on his right arm to cover the tattooed name of an old flame. His wife thinks it's a good idea.

He is Lee Trevino, the Mexican grave-digger's grandson, who became American Open champion in his first full season on the professional circuit.

That win was an impudent contradiction to the years of dedication Ben Hogan endured to earn this and other accolades. It whipped the carpet from beneath the Big Three — Arnold Palmer, Jack Nicklaus and Gary Player. Somebody even called it an inspired accident.

Trevino's subsequent career has been scrutinised in terms of whether it could disprove the fluke theory. His initial achievement was worth 800,000 dollars to him in contracts and other business. Not bad for a man who was so broke the year before that his wife lent him the money to enter the American Open.

But somehow he undermined his own achievement with an off-hand and and clownish manner. The quotable quotes are already legend: "How can a Mexican win something like this? I'll have to be Spanish! I think I'll buy the Alamo and give it back to Mexico!" It was an image that would rebound on him for, wherever he played, people expected the jokes. His golf was not enough. And he confessed after one tournament: "People think I joke to relieve the tension. But really I do it because the crowd expect it."

Historically, Trevino is of great importance for he symbolised a fundamental change in American golf. The game had been invaded by tough young men, uninhibited by reverence for reputations and sustained by an almost tangible confidence in their own powers.

Right: Trevino the Clown has his serious side — he turned down his chance to play in this year's Masters in Augusta, Georgia, some say, because no negroes had been invited to compete.

44

Trevino said at the time: "It's not a question of a good golf swing any more. It's the putting stroke. And that means guts. I've got guts."

Nobody doubted it. His earlier life was documented proof of the claim. His parents separated when he was a boy and he lived with his grandfather. At fifteen, he had left school and was working as a shoe shine boy. Later he got a job at a driving range in Dallas and hustled unsuspecting customers with bets that he could beat them round a par-three course using only a beer bottle for a club. He never lost.

At best his golf swing is functional. It grew from his boyhood habit of hitting crab apples with a stick. A small man, he is naturally a flat swinger. And the strong winds of Texas, where he learned to play, produced a low-flighted boring shot not normally successful on the watered fairways on the American tour, where the emphasis is on targetry.

He has a wide stance but, like Arnold Palmer, he keeps his left hand moving towards the target longer than most other professionals—a clear sign he is forestalling the dangers of a hook from an overpowerful right hand.

By instinct he is a gambler with a refreshing perspective on money that only a man who has been poor can enjoy. He explained his philosophy thus: "There's nothing else to do with money except enjoy life. I get more fun out of it because I was poor once. I don't take anything for granted. Money has always been my incentive even when I was a caddy to pay for the family groceries."

When he won the Hawaiian Open, he handed over the $10,000 prize money to the widow and children of a golf professional who had drowned in a swimming accident. Even when he lost a six-stroke lead in the last three holes of the 1969 Alcan Golfer of the Year championship—and with it, the £23,000 first prize—he joked with the crowd: "Hell, what do I want all that money for? I can't spend what I've got now!"

He has a special affection for children. He smokes cigarettes but refuses to be photographed smoking "because it's a bad example for the kids." At one British Open, he distributed his magnificent and colourful golf wardrobe to local youngsters. His parties for under-privileged children in America are legendary and he even brings them by the bus-load to golf tournaments.

"A man works hard all his life to raise money to enjoy that life. I want to spread it around a little bit. Sure I want to be one of the big golf stars. But golf isn't everything. When I go to other countries to play, I want to see the people as well."

Left: They asked him if he studied the weaknesses of a Golf Course when he played it and he answered: "I ain't that smart. If I was I'd be a lawyer!" But Trevino's antics, like his disgust at the putt that wouldn't drop, sometimes works against him and his concentration.

"BUFFALO BILL"

BILLY CASPER is a man with a mission. He is now quite convinced that destiny has some special place for him in golf, not for any personal gratification but simply to spread his evangelistic work.

Cynics suggest that if this is the psychological gimmick he needs to keep his nerve and rhythm against the gnawing demands of tournament golf, then don't knock it. With other people, drink, women and purple hearts have the same therapeutic effect. But with Casper it goes deeper. Even though Palmer was seven strokes ahead with nine holes left of the 1966 American Open, Casper claims he "knew" that he, himself, was going to be champion.

Sure enough, Palmer threw it away as only he could and the title fell to the relentless efficiency of William Casper. Palmer denied any divine intervention. He was just too greedy and took too many chances trying to break Ben Hogan's record instead of being content with an Open championship.

This is the essential difference between these two players who both turned professional in 1954. Casper has always played within himself and never allowed the pressure of the moment to lure him into a rash decision.

He has made a lot of money this way and became the second man to earn a million dollars prize money. Palmer was the first. But such strategy doesn't win many big championships which demand that a man go out and grab them and not simply hope that everybody falls down to leave him standing alone in the rubble.

The paradox may be that the personal philosophy which now governs Casper's life has lessened his obsession with things temporal—and that includes winning championships. His wife, Shirley, who was first converted to the Mormon faith, says: "When Billy became a Mormon, golf—for its own sake—

48

seemed to lose its importance. Before that, he knew nothing else. But the strange thing is that because it mattered less, it took tension off him. He started to win more."

Thus he meekly accepted 40 disastrous strokes over Augusta's front nine holes when the Master's title was close enough to touch. Nobody in that silent crowd will ever forget the nonchalant way he took two shots to get out of a bunker and never reached the green. It could have been a weekend hacker — not a man with a chance to prove wrong all those who said he could never win this big one.

Still, he came second and his equable countenance faltered only once — as George Archer donned the green jacket of Masters champion.

Afterwards he confessed: "I have a strong feeling I am intended to win the Masters. It is the sort of feeling I had against Palmer in 1966. Some achievements are inevitable. That million dollar target for instance. I knew I should reach it. I feel the same about the Masters. But it's not life or death. The trouble in golf is that if you try too hard, you defeat the purpose."

Let others try a bit too hard and over-stretch themselves. Casper is waiting to pounce.

Lee Trevino was six strokes clear with only three holes separating him from the £23,000 Alcan prize at Portland in 1969. Incredibly, he lost them all in a hideous procession of errors. Guess who picked up the cheque? William Casper.

Casper is a complex character. At one time he weighed almost sixteen stone and was a highly-strung, tempestuous young man. His fatness, it was diagnosed, came from allergies to certain foods. He went on a special diet which included buffalo meat and gave rise to his nickname and trademark "Buffalo Bill". But he shed almost four stone. His temperament improved and was soothed even more by his growing religious beliefs.

He still pays meticulous attention to his health — an oxygen mask in the golf bag to combat industrial fumes, a conviction that long sleeve pullovers don't make him sweat, and he always checks to discover what pesticides have been used on a course he is to play. He knows the signs and at Royal Lytham in 1969, observed birds swooping close to the ground: "That's good. It means the pesticides aren't strong. Otherwise the birds wouldn't come."

He has won *almost* as many tournaments as Palmer. His simple, quick no-nonsense swing will certainly endure longer than Palmer's punishing fury. His swing really begins when he takes the club from the bag. He wastes no time — half a practice swing and a quick delivery at the ball. If the routine is broken, the club goes back in the bag and it starts all over again.

He is held to be the best putter in the world and admits: "As a boy, I spent more time on the putting green. I didn't like all that walking round the course. But I really don't think I get more putts than anybody else. It comes and it

49

And the prophecy came true: Casper said he felt destined to win the American Masters — three months before it happened.

goes. Some days, there's just no way to get the ball into the hole."

Lurking somewhere at the back of his mind is a puzzled resentment that his achievements have not earned him the sort of acclaim Palmer has been accorded. Of course he hasn't won the championships Palmer has. But he says: "It's wrong to measure success simply on the number of championships a man has won. There are far too many important tournaments around for a man to be judged simply on the big championships." But even without titles, Palmer still has the edge in immediate public impact. And Casper's change of manager — to a man Casper met in Las Vegas who had looked after singer Trini Lopez — was probably prompted by this desire to find more appeal. But Casper, as a personality, has a worthiness not immediately apparent — not in the Palmer sock-it-to-them fashion. Out of golf clothes, he has the grey-flannelled manner of an important company executive. His dress, as with his manner and golf, is always sober and conservative.

"I know this religious image makes me out to be some kind of Holy Joe," he says. "People are looking for weaknesses — whether I show anger on the course if things go wrong. They know what I am and they're looking. Every day I say a prayer that I won't let myself go. Sometimes, it's a strain."

But his philosophy is consistent. He feels a man should stand up and be counted—golfer or not. Thus he went to Vietnam to entertain the troops. He adopted three orphaned children much younger than his own three. All his spare time is given to addressing religious meetings.

The evening before he won the 1970 Los Angeles Open play-off, which took his prize money over a million dollars—he was already a millionaire from his business interests—Casper drove one hundred miles to address a meeting. The same thing happened the night before he beat Palmer in a play-off for the Open in 1966. It could be coincidence. But to Casper, it is evidence that somebody up there not only likes him—but is prepared to show it.

In this year's Masters he took a seven at one hole and said, "I wasn't going to throw it away for the second time." He recovered and beat Gene Littler in a play-off.

Peter Townsend

DANCING
GOLFERS

Gay Brewer

Clive Clark

Billy Casper

Brian Barnes

Peter Green

Tommy Horton

"THE DUKE"

MICHAEL BONALLACK is probably the last of the breed, an amateur who is one of the best golfers in Britain.

It is doubtful whether anybody after him will ever reach that degree of skill again, while still preferring to play the game for fun. One reason for his undisputed position in amateur golf is that the younger men who might have matured to challenge him, stay only a short time before turning to the professional game.

If Bonallack had chosen to follow them, it would have been because he wanted to prove he was good enough and not for any dreams of a fortune. That, sufficient for his needs, he already had from a large family business of which he is a director. But now, at the age of thirty-four, he feels it is too late to think of professionalism and says: "When I was young enough, I wasn't good enough. Now perhaps I'm good enough, but not young enough."

Bonallack set about diligently changing his style which was aimed to rid him of a dangerous pick-up on the backswing and a virtual lunge at the ball. Next season, he reappeared looking slightly changed but as soon as the pressures came back, so did the old Bonallack style. Yet he still won. The lessons did him some technical good but their true worth was probably to sharpen the urge, retain the focus, of a man who might have got bored with success simply through constant acquaintance.

Not surprisingly, he is cast in the same mould as the two men he idolises, Joe Carr and Billy Joe Patton. Both were world-class golfers, yet both remained amateurs and became institutions in their own countries — Patton in the United States and Carr throughout the British Isles. Patton almost won an American championship against the world's top professionals. And Carr came close to winning several major tournaments against the professionals — including the British Open.

54

Bonallack says his swing looks like he is shovelling coal—because it is so ugly. But it makes him one of the best amateurs in the world.

Bonallack has won the individual world amateur title and will continue to accumulate personal honours. But two goals are firmly fixed in his mind; winning the American Amateur and being in a successful Walker Cup side. Both would raise the status of British amateur golf and Bonallack now thinks in terms of what he can give back to the game. And he could do no better than these.

His golf swing, he readily admits, looks like he is shovelling coal. Yet he dominates the game to such an overwhelming extent that he has been named

"The Duke", partly because of a resemblance to Prince Philip, but also because it sums up the awed reverence in which he is held by contemporaries.

Even so, it is arguable whether his individual style, which is so unpredictable that he developed an infallible recovery game and putting touch to compensate, could stand the constant rigours of tournament golf which expose every flaw. As an amateur, Bonallack's only concern is reputation or glory. It is not a way of living. And this has given him a sort of mental freedom to play his own perilous way without the need for a repeating, functional "money swing".

Without question, he is the best man with a putter, professional or amateur, within fifteen feet of the hole. It is a disaster for him to miss. His awareness of this ability makes him a devastating opponent in matchplay.

He has perfected the art of "scrambling", getting his score without playing copybook golf. Bonallack can carve his own tortuous path around a golf course and still emerge as the winner.

Whether he plays the sublime or the ridiculous, Bonallack can still win. He regards this kind of determination as the most important quality in a golfer. "I would rather a man had this quality than the best golf swing in the world," he says. "In a tight corner, it's his determination, and not his technique, that will get him out of trouble. I know I've got an awful swing. But people have been telling me that since I won my first title eighteen years ago."

When Gordon Cosh, later to become a top Walker Cup player, first saw the swing without knowing the owner, he asked: "Who is that? And how does he get a handicap low enough to play in this?" They led him off and explained that he was talking about Bonallack, the defending champion.

Bonallack was the first man for thirty years to defend successfully the British Amateur title. He missed his chance of a hat-trick in English titles in 1969 but even then had a total of five to his credit.

No victory was more cruel, yet magnificent, than his annihilation of opponent – and course – in the 1968 English championship final at Ganton. He beat Michael Kelley by 12 and 11 and reduced the tough Yorkshire course to an embarrassing 61 strokes in the morning round. But he has endured his share of disasters and none hurt more than losing a five-hole lead with only six to play against Bruce Fleisher, the American champion, in the 1969 Walker Cup match at Milwaukee.

Fleisher was the glamour-boy of the American side. He wore bell-bottomed trousers and red-and-white shoes. Off the course, he sported a string of beads around his neck and greeted everybody with: "Peace and Love, brother!" But underneath that "flower power" image, Fleisher had an iron-willed determination. He launched a furious counterattack which saw Bonallack lose five in a row and narrowly escape with a halved hole on the last green. The Englishman could not have been more shattered had he lost.

Out of season, Bonallack is reluctant to play golf. His wife, Angela, herself a former English champion and Curtis Cup player, says that he has to be persuaded to go round a golf course—even for the exercise. Yet, in season, no man is subject to a more punishing competitive schedule with no more purpose than the exhilaration of a challenge.

"I still feel that I can improve," he says. "If I didn't, there would be no point in playing the game or carrying on. I might just as well give up. But I'm convinced that my best golf has still to come."

Two years ago, with all those titles to his credit, he went for secret golf lessons during the winter to change his golf swing. His tutor was Leslie King, who served an exclusive clientele in the basement of a West End block of flats. King told Bonallack he would have to forget all he ever knew about a golf swing. "What you've got now," said King, "is a ruddy awful mess!"

The Bonallack "eye-ball" putting method—crouched very low over ball. It looks odd, but the "Duke" rarely misses.

"WONDER BOY"

HE was sitting alone, deep in thought, as the aircraft droned towards London. An hour ago, he had missed first place and £2,000.

Quite suddenly he spoke, to nobody in particular: "Damn it! I was watching the wrong man. How in hell did Shade slip in there? If only I'd known it was him. I was thinking about Cristy. Damn it!"

To Bernard Gallacher, the loss of Carrolls International's £2,000 first prize didn't hurt as much as being beaten. And somehow it hurt more because Ronnie Shade, a fellow Scot, had done it. But while this off-stage episode demonstrated the young Scot's grim desire to be top man, it reflected the phenomenal standards he had come to expect of himself. For at this time, he had been a touring professional for only six months.

By the end of his first season, he had won two major tournaments and was runner-up in another three. He played a vital role in Britain's historic Ryder Cup tie with the United States and beat Lee Trevino on that crucial final afternoon.

He played for Scotland in the World Cup, became Britain's leading home money winner with almost £7,000 and came under the international management of Cleveland lawyer Mark McCormack, who also numbers Arnold Palmer, Jack Nicklaus and Gary Player among his clients. All this, within eighteen months of leaving school.

Several theories were advanced for this incredible debut. The old professionals said he didn't know how difficult golf could be. He hadn't been around long enough. They reckoned that his impudent aggression would evaporate the more he played the professional game.

Peter Alliss confessed: "He frightens me with his sheer confidence. He charges a putt six feet past the hole then calmly drops it coming back. He expects to hole everything. I hope for his sake it lasts. Golf tests the confidence as much as it does technique. Perhaps more so."

The other theory of his success is really an alternative aspect of this point. Peter Thomson advanced the thought that the bigger 1.68-inch golf ball, compulsory in British tournaments, was more difficult to control. Scoring therefore relied more heavily on good recovery work and sound putting. In both departments, Gallacher's confidence and technique were more than sufficient.

But success itself, coming so early, presented its own problem for the 20-year-old Edinburgh golfer. "When you've come top, there's nothing you can do to improve. If I don't come top again I suppose people will say it was just a lucky fluke in the first place," he said. "Anyway, the worst thing I can do is look back on the old glories. That's all past. I know the pressure will always be on me to do well. Just to prove it wasn't luck. But I also know I will run into a bad patch because no golfer, not even the best, has ever escaped without one. I won't be disappointed if I'm not Number One again."

Gallacher has learned the painful way that success brings with it other responsibilities, which extend beyond simply producing the best score possible. He thundered from the last green at Royal Lytham during the 1969 Open after a bad round and uttered thoughts about quitting.

The press immediately took it up and he was advised to go back and tell them that he had spoken in a fit of depression and didn't mean it. But even that served only to add to the reports the next day. All important sportsmen face the unfair, but inevitable burden, of being quoted even if what they say is ill-timed. Gallacher said it was pointless going to play in the U.S. Masters because neither he nor anybody else from Britain could expect to do very well in just one week.

But, in his innocence, he had missed the point. An invitation to the exclusive U.S. Masters in Augusta reflects a person's international status and ranks marginally second to a command to attend Buckingham Palace. Once again, he was advised to reconsider.

But he remains inflexible on some principles and refused to accept an invitation to the Nigerian Open because "it seemed totally irrelevant and wrong to be playing golf for £1,000 when, down the road, people were starving."

"I am conscious now that I have to behave myself," he says. "I just can't go out any more around the town with my old pals from Bathgate. Yet I don't want them to think I've got no time for them. But it's difficult to open your mouth without sounding like you're bragging—when you can talk about places like Singapore and Africa because you've been there; or you've paid more for a suit than they earn in a month. I don't want to grow away from them—but I suppose I will."

Of his tournament contemporaries he says: "I know that a lot of the boys are better strikers than me. But they don't think any better. All the way round the course, I talk myself into doing the right things. They worry over a small putt. But I say to myself that I cannot really miss."

When Gary Player was asked to comment on Gallacher he said that the young Scot was a fine pitcher and putter but had the worse grip he had ever seen. If he wanted to win championships he would have to change it. "Have you ever seen a great golfer with a bad grip?" asked Player. "Gallacher is an excellent fighter and if he works on his game he can become a great player."

Undoubtedly Gallacher's grip, which earned him success, might not satisfy the purists. He uses an interlocking grip, as does Jack Nicklaus. While there is no harm in this, Gallacher has a tendency to let the right hand slide under the club with a resultant roll into the shot, shutting the face and causing a hook.

But it was Max Faulkner, young Gallacher's mentor, who provided the most appropriate comment: "Considering what Bernard's done with a bad grip, I wonder if he would teach it to me?"

Below: Gallacher's strength is his cool nerve and steady hand on a putting green. But the older professionals wonder how long his confidence will last; Gary Player said Gallacher's grip was the worst he had ever seen (right). But he reckoned the young Scot had the best potential in Britain.

U.K. RECORDS

The lowest score recorded on an 18-hole course was 55 (15 under bogey) at Woolacombe by professional A. E. Smith on 1 January 1936.

The lowest score recorded on a course over 6,000 yards is 58 by Harry Weetman, British Ryder Cup golfer, at Croham Hurst Course (6,171 yards) in Croydon on 30 January 1956.

In a first class professional tournament, the lowest score recorded for a course of more than 6,000 yards was 61 (29 out, 32 in) by Thomas Bruce Haliburton in the Spalding Tournament of 1952 at Worthing, Sussex.

Peter Butler equalled the 18-hole tournament record on 4 July 1967 on the Old Course at Sunningdale, Berkshire, during the Bowmaker Tournament.

The 9-hole lowest score record is 28—scored by John Panton at Harrogate, Yorkshire, in the Swallow-Penfold Tournament in 1952.

HIGHEST SCORES

Twenty-one is the highest score for a single hole in the British Open—this "record" occurred at Prestwick in 1860.

Nineteen strokes for a par-4 hole (the 16th) were carded by Ray Ainsley of Ojai, California, during the second round of the U.S. Open Tournament at Cherry Hills Country Club in Denver, Colorado (10 June 1938).

Worse yet, Hans Merrell of Mogadore, Ohio, scored *19 strokes* on the 15th hole (par-3) during the third round of the Bing Crosby National Tournament at Cypress Point Club in Del Monte, California (17th January 1959).

The Chevalier von Cittern scored the magnificent sum of *316 strokes* for *18 holes* at Biarritz, France, in 1888.

These are scores that most golfers and fans would prefer to forget . . . probably on the theory that "it could happen to anyone!"

THE U.S. OPEN TOURNAMENT

The United States Open Golf Championship was first started in 1894.

Jack Nicklaus scored the lowest 72-hole aggregate—275 (75,67,72 and 65) on the Lower Course (which is 7,015 yards) at Baltusrol Country Club at Springfield, New Jersey, during June 1968.

During the tournament the lowest score recorded has been 64—achieved three times by Lee Mackey, Jr., at the Merion Country Club in Ardmore, Pennsylvania (8 June 1950); by Tommy Jacobs at the Congressional Country Club, Washington, D.C. (19 June 1964); and by Rives McBee at the Olympic Country Club in San Francisco, California (17 June 1966).

THE LUNATIC FRINGE OF THE OLD BOY GOLFERS

WHAT is a man supposed to think about when his hands, wrists, forearms and elbows go wooden with cold; when his feet slop loosely in shoes over-flowing with icy melted sleet; and he is faced with a ten-foot putt to keep the game alive? Meanwhile, an ample limousine with motor running and heater going full blast stands beside the green ready to take him away from his ordeal back to the survival area, to the shelter of the clubhouse and the promise of unlimited stimulants.

The golfer studies the line at length and rams the ball manfully into the back of the hole. He straightens, looks wistfully at the sanctuary of the motor car, then moves on to the next tee. The question is, does he have any coherent thoughts at all? Is his stubborn persistence to a cause the result of an act of will, or is it, like good manners, something dinned into him when young?

Well, I will let you into a secret by telling you that it is neither of these. It is simply the tradition of a strange near-religious golfing rite, called "The Halford-Hewitt", that the show must go on and that every member of the side is expected to do his duty, even if that duty means prolonging exposure to arctic conditions for the sake of salvaging half a point for an already beaten team.

The Halford-Hewitt is the old-boy competition to end all old-boy com-petitions, one of the last remaining bastions of foursome (alternate strokes) golf, played annually at Deal and Royal St. Georges Sandwich.

Its importance to those who have played in it year after year ranks fully as high as any Open or Amateur championship. Places in the team are coveted more than any neighbour's wife, and for these a perpetual struggle goes on between the generations. Old campaigners refuse to accept the effect of passing years and a decision to replace a senior with a junior has repercussions as severe as a cabinet reshuffle. If and when a young lad, fresh from school, agrees unwittingly to join the team, he is soon made conscious of his res-ponsibilities. In his first match he will be surprised, and perhaps a trifle flat-tered to be followed round by a small gathering of shooting-stick squatters, but woe betide him if he fluffs a chip or misses a short putt at a crucial moment.

The tongues wag like larks in spring: old so and so would have put that one

in, they mutter among themselves, and the news is relayed round the course by sand-dune and umbrella telegraph.

On the other hand, for the bold young entrant to play too well is to overdo it and to take all the fun away. It is traditional that the match be taken so seriously, that to strike the ball clean and true from tee to green and occasionally to hole for a birdie is considered slightly off: the person concerned obviously fails to appreciate the importance of the occasion.

If one were to suggest a proper and acceptable way of, say, playing the nineteenth at Deal, the hole would go something like this:

On the drive, player A should be so certain that his head is kept anchored (this is for the benefit of those watching from the club house) that, with rhythm lost, he hits one high off the top of the club. The ball will clear the rough, just, and come to rest not more than one hundred and fifty yards from the tee in a slightly scruffy lie on the fairway.

Pity the man who is left with the ball sitting up, because then he must make a choice between a brassie to clear the brook, or an iron short of it: Better to leave each other continually with at least some element of difficulty so that an excuse is available and acceptable for a miscue.

Player B can now do the "sensible thing", thinning the ball quail high for another hundred and odd yards, whereupon he should mutter the standard explanation for this nastily executed stab, "as good as a better".

Player A, now faced, in a moment of truth, with getting the ball airborne over the water and onto the green, selects two clubs more than he needs and sends it sailing fifteen yards into the rough beyond: on the basis, I always imagine, of that sound advice to the young—"if you can't be good, be careful!"

Player B now has a swish in the long grass and, more by luck than anything, trickles it within ten feet of the hole, and an appreciative round of applause reminds him of the many times he has thus proved his mettle in a crisis.

Player A now hits a firm putt on the line chosen in consultation with B, but, just too firm, it hits the rim and spins out. Again it is more than a man's reputation is worth to leave the ball short on line.

So the side takes six at a comparatively simple par four, but honour is satisfied. It may mean losing and the need for a semblance of dejection on the way back to the locker-room, but it is only a show. Both A and B know in their hearts that they did the right thing and should be certain of their places next year.

Left: Even mad dogs find shelter when its snowing. But nothing keeps an Englishman from his golf even if he has to dress in Eskimo style. Alan Holmes makes his effort in the President's Putter at Rye—an annual outbreak of madness among Oxford and Cambridge players always arranged for the desperate weeks of January (golf is not considered much of a summer sport among the Oxbridge Brigade).

G—E

GOLFING CELEBRITIES

Above: The difference, as England footballer Bobby Charlton will tell you, is how they don't throw toilet rolls and pennies when you hit a bad shot at golf! Right: Comedian Bruce Forsyth is a golf nut, but plays many matches to raise funds for charities.

"007" looks worried. Not Goldfinger—just a shot that doesn't seem to be going where Sean Connery intended!

Golf always gets the last laugh—even from someone like Dickie Henderson and Eric Sykes.

HAVE CLUB, WILL TRAVEL

MAURICE BEMBRIDGE has clubs and will travel. He is one of the mavericks of professional golf who will turn up in Bangkok or Birmingham if the money is right. Even in his early days, this 25-year-old Midlander knew that he would have to travel the world if he was to be different from the hundreds of young players who dreamt of success.

It was not enough to stay home during winter and hit a few practice shots because other, more venturesome, golfers were stealing time and experience somewhere else in the world. And it was not just golf experience. The international performer must be able to adapt to other demands without any effect on his golf. He must shrug off the time differences of jet travel, the vagaries of diet and climate wherever he happens to be.

If he cannot endure the draining humidity of Kuala Lumpur or the biting winds of Troon—without effect to his golf swing—then he is *not* equipped to join the international set.

Thus Bembridge roams the world. From October until the following April, he is somewhere in between Australia, the Far East, India and Africa. And the first sign of spring in his hometown of Worksop is Bembridge's arrival at the bank with all manner of currency in prize money—Hong Kong dollars, American dollars, Australian dollars and some from Malaya, India and Africa.

"It's an investment in myself," he says, "quite apart from really stealing another season on the fellows who stay at home in Britain during the winter. After all, our British tour lasts about six months and I spend that amount of time playing golf out of the country.

Maurice Bembridge: "You don't get better just wishing it would happen."

The world traveller copes with all problems in a relaxed and cool style—even the bunkers.

72

"The more I travel now, the more I will acquire the techniques that go to make up an international player with a future. I'm not in a hurry. I want my progress to the top to come in easy stages—so that I don't lose what I've learned."

This solitary pilgrimage round the world gives a man something else, a priceless strength of will, an independence of spirit, that perhaps ultimately separates a winner from the rest.

"I'm in Australia and suddenly it's all gone wrong," he says. "I just can't play. I've earned $84 from three tournaments. And I'm sitting in a hotel, a blister on my right heel, a touch of tonsilitis and a cholera injection that's playing up. I just want to go home. But I know I mustn't quit. I must play through it all—because that's my business.

"This life also teaches a sort of professional detachment that probably borders on cruelty. I came in after one round and moaned like hell about my luck. Peter Thomson was there and he said, 'Thank's for telling us your troubles, but do you realise that nobody here really cares?' And he was right. Your luck is no better or worse than anybody else's. So keep quiet.

"You learn never to assume anything. In Singapore I didn't read a notice board which said you could stop play during those torrential showers. I played on and missed a green. It cost me a stroke and about $300 prize money.

"In Kuala Lumpur, you must remember to take salt tablets. You must eat well and drink a lot of soft drinks to combat the humidity. Otherwise you get cramp, dizziness and even faint. You've got to have a cast-iron stomach because you're going to eat all sorts of food—some of it good, some terrible. But it mustn't affect you.

"And then there are the penalties of travel. The midnight arrival in Calcutta with forms to sign, officials to see and a piece of luggage that's gone on to Bahrein and will not be back until the tournament is over. The curfew in Singapore. The riots in Manila, where, even when it's quiet, you cannot move more than a few yards from the hotel.

"But from it all, you're learning the professional way," he says. "You learn how to work a golf ball round a golf course. Not brilliant flash-bang stuff, but the kind of way that makes money. You learn the safe sides to miss a green because you're not going to hit every one. You learn to play a ball short when the wind's blowing from the right otherwise you're going to run through the green. You are playing a percentage game because you're there to make money."

That knack, Bembridge has acquired. In 1969, after his first global pilgrimage he ended the year with £11,000, the British PGA Matchplay title and a half-share in the Sumrie Four-Ball tournament. His winter tour costs about £2,000 and it is a sign of his growing education that he always covers his costs—and then some.

"THE SWINGER"

IN both senses, Raymond Floyd is a formidable swinger. His golf technique earned him the American PGA champion's title at the age of twenty-six. And nowhere was this triumph more joyously received than in the topless nightclubs of San Francisco where Floyd is something of a local boy.

He is a character in the great Walter Hagen tradition, in that he can raise hell until dawn and still go out and play great golf. As he explained: "I've got great powers of recovery. I need only a few hours' sleep. I don't turn into a pumpkin at midnight. Some golfers relax by hunting and fishing. But if you have to carry a gun where I go, you're at the wrong party!"

His escapades are already part of the textbook. He lost £800 just passing an hour in a seaside casino during one British Open. His name has been linked with several Hollywood film starlets. One girl-friend was ordered from the course during an American championship because she was scantily-clad.

Floyd served his apprenticeship to the gay life under such masters as Doug Sanders and Al Besselink, but refutes the theory that this early influence prevented him from becoming as important in golf as Jack Nicklaus. "That's nonsense," he says. "I was fortunate to win a tournament in my first season but there just weren't as many good players around as there are now. Anyway, I didn't spend all that much time with Sanders and Besselink and we drifted apart. I couldn't play well at all if I didn't go to parties."

Behind the hell-raiser image is a formidable golf talent. He was a junior American champion and perfected his swing through hours of practice on a driving range owned by his father. He has always known about the pressures of golf and explained: "If a guy came up to me and said he'd play for a hundred dollars if I gave him ten strokes, I'd say I'd give him twelve strokes and play for a thousand dollars. I'd find his choking price and when he gets on the course, he can't breathe!"

Until the 1969 American PGA championship, he seemed saddled with the "Pretty Boy" Floyd image — attractive to watch but irresolute in his desire to win the big one. All that changed dramatically in the most acute test of skill and courage a sportsman has ever faced. Not only was Gary Player charging purposefully after him for that title in the last round, but both men were ringed by armed police against possible violence from demonstrators. The violence never came and though Floyd felt the pressure of his big moment, his powers of recovery on a golf course took him to his first major title.

Left: The man who wants to be a millionaire by the time he's 30.

Some said he was the natural successor to Jack Nicklaus, but Floyd decided to enjoy himself first.

His one moment of serious trouble all week had been self-inflicted. He criticised the slowness of a veteran player in an earlier round and the attack appeared in print. No sooner were the first editions on the street than Floyd was called to apologise. Later that day, notices appeared round the clubhouse carrying his statement.

"I've always lived by one standard," he says. "I never want to do anything to make my parents ashamed of me. And so far, I haven't. First, I'm trying to be a super golfer. And I think I'm on the right track. I never train seriously. I'm not a hard worker. But I want to be a millionaire by the time I'm thirty."

CADDIES

THE emancipation of the British golf caddie was made complete when Jock Allan took over a suite in the Carlton Towers while his employer, Billy Casper, spent a few days in Switzerland.

But then Casper treats his men well. Allan, who used to work in a casino until he followed Casper's example and became a Mormon, also had the use of an eight-seater limousine—complete with chauffeur. "I don't see anything strange in all this," says Allan whose wife and children live in Southport while he follows the summer tour. "I'm as good as any other man. People seem to think that caddies are a different form of life. I don't sleep in bunkers. And I don't booze every penny I get. I can pay my way."

Allan is one of the handful of top caddies in Britain—the men whom any visiting American wants to employ when competing in Britain. These caddies know the major courses and they are quick to assess the style of their employer—in temperament and golf.

Southport has become the "caddie capital" and most of these men work at Royal Birkdale. But they could never have been classified as fitting the old vagabond, almost Runyonesque, image of a golf caddie.

Jackie Leigh, for example, works exclusively for the Australian Peter Thomson and has won two British Open titles with him. He is an ex-wrestler, runs a small coal-delivery business and is a member of a golf club.

Alfie Fyles, a painter and decorator, is probably Britain's best known—and highest paid —caddie. Gary Player retains his services exclusively while in Britain and Gay Brewer is reputed to have tipped him £1,000 when he won the Alcan Golfer of the Year championship in successive years.

"It's a mistake to think that a caddie's two duties are to keep the clubs clean and his mouth shut," says Fyles. "I can save any golfer at least three shots a round just by giving him advice. When Gay Brewer won at St. Andrews, he said afterwards he couldn't have done it without me.

"You get to know what your man wants. Gary Player likes me to stand about eight yards from him when he plays his shot. He wants the flagstick out as soon as he strikes his putt. He doesn't want me to talk to him. He'll talk to me.

"Sometimes he might ask me what club I think he should take. But I know

Alfie Fyles, citizen of Southport, the caddies' capital, embraces his client Gary Player on Carnoustie's last green as the South African wins the British Open. And Jimmy Dickinson, Jack Nicklaus's caddie, offers his congratulations.

he's already made up his mind and just wants some reassurance. After all, he's one of the best golfers in the world. If he doesn't know what club—who does?"

Most top tournament golfers employ a regular caddie, simply because they do not want to run the risk of getting an incompetent who might distract them or even ruin their chances. Maurice Bembridge, for example, was disqualified from a PGA championship because a caddie slipped a new ball to the ground when Bembridge's was lost. The golfer discovered the switch and reported the crime. There was no alternative but to disqualify him from the tournament because he played the new ball before the discovery.

Peter Alliss is always teamed with "Little Jimmy" who also gets the occasional bonus from his employer's extensive wardrobe. Dave Thomas employs "Ginger" Finch. Neil Coles is attended by Arthur "Chingy" Maidment who has been known to reverse roles and give his employer a severe ticking-off after a bad shot. Jock Allan has worked for Brian Barnes.

Just how much they earn remains a close secret. But the average deal which would attract these top men is about a basic £20 a week plus a percentage of whatever prize money is won. And, as they work only for the top men, this could put their weekly income around £30.

But these are the elite who regard themselves as professionals. The game still has its core of character caddies—like "Mad Mac" who always wore a raincoat, no shirt, and peered at every putt through binoculars from which the glass had been removed. His constant advice was: "Hit this putt slightly straight, sir!"

There was also a great caddie called "Wingy" Pearson. He had only one arm, and once brandished rosary beads at a colleague and declared: "Your man will take 80 tomorrow!" Sure enough, the man did and "Wingy" Pearson's rosary beads became the dreaded weapon of the professional circuit.

Another circuit caddie devised a very special way of passing the winter until the next season. He issued dud cheques of sufficient value to earn himself about five months at Her Majesty's centrally-heated, well-fed pleasure. Towards the end of his term, he would write to a golf official asking for a fixture list so that he knew exactly where to rejoin the professional tour.

Jock Allan says: "You won't find top caddies getting involved in trouble. They know that the top golfers would drop them straight away. And nobody's daft enough to give up the sort of money these men pay."

The top caddie can assemble a clientele that is adequate reflection of his own merit. Willie Aitchison has worked for Joe Carr, Michael Bonallack, Roberto De Vicenzo and Lee Trevino (and broke a leg while working for the Mexican during the Ryder Cup). And it is sufficient comment on the caddie's importance that when Aitchison decided to carry for Trevino and not De Vicenzo, he got headlines on the sports page in most national papers.

THE ROYAL AND ANCIENT GOLF CLUB OF ST. ANDREWS

THERE are many and varied aspects to any monarchy. Among them is the role of paternal head of state and that of resplendent super-representative for impressing the outside world. Just as important, perhaps, in our democracy, the monarch ensures that this exalted position, with all its status and ultimate responsibility, does not fall into the wrong hands.

Such, in the world of golf, is the role of the Royal and Ancient Golf Club of St. Andrews.

How exactly and why the R & A, as it is now commonly called, developed from a simple gathering of sportsmen into the most influential body in the great game of golf, is a story little less remarkable in its way than the history of chance and circumstance which brought Elizabeth II herself to the throne. They have in common, however, that, despite the inherited nature of their office, they both continue to receive most people's goodwill and approval.

This is not to say that they think themselves infallible — a number of headless Kings and Queens can vouch for the vulnerable nature of that way of thinking, so it is not by any divine right that the 1,750 members of the R & A act as the governing authority for the game of golf throughout most of the world.

In the early days, it is true, it seems that they rather took it upon themselves to set standards, develop rules and encourage competition, but it is also evident that, subsequently, throughout the two hundred and odd years of their jurisdiction, nobody has had either cause to complain of their performance nor good reason to think they could do the job better themselves.

The story began on 14 May 1754 when twenty-two Fife noblemen and gentlemen formed "the Society of St. Andrews Golfers"; which is exactly what they remained until 1834, when King William IV became patron of the club and permitted the Royal title.

So far as one can gather these pioneers were not seeking a place in the history books. Rather they seemed set upon competing amongst themselves for a Silver Club, no less, the winner to be called "Captain of Golf".

The Royal and Ancient Golf Club of St Andrews.

Nor is it suggested that they were the first golfers. Records show that the game was being played in Scotland as far back as 1413 with the earliest reference to golf at St. Andrews dated 1552. Furthermore the original minutes of the foundation meeting of the club refer specifically to St. Andrews as the "Alma Mater of the Golf", so our active clubmen were not altogether breaking new ground.

It would, of course, be a fascinating exercise to turn back in time and actually glimpse those early players battling with the game and the same moods of elation and frustration as we know today.

One envies future generations the libraries of film material they will inherit to compare champion with champion, and duffer with duffer. For us, the links, appropriately called, provide about the only experience we can in any way share, since the original "Old Course", covered all but the same narrow strip of natural golfing country which tested the modern professionals in the 1970 Open Championship.

Originally it consisted of 22 holes, 11 out and 11 in. Having played 11 it was a simple matter to turn about and play back to the same holes from the opposite direction. Possibly this accounts for the random siting of bunkers the like of which no self respecting golf architect would dare to plan, just as he would be hard put to find a buyer for the next development of the Old Course greens, which consisted in duplicating the holes. This little eccentricity is to be enjoyed still and makes any visit worthwhile if only to have the merest possibility of actually holing a seventy-yard putt. Even more accentric to our way of thinking was the absence of a separate teeing ground, the rule being that you "drove" off the green itself within two club-lengths

1384 — Golf, or Bandy-ball.

Mansell

SOME GOLFERS OF THE PAST

Mansell   Mansell   Mansell

Cock of the Green.   *A Young Dutch Golfer.*   *Mary, Queen of Scots.*

of the hole. The divots and sand round the cup must plainly have presented putting problems but I suppose everything is relative. Presumably there were compensations: such as the ever-widening target which resulted from the common practice of scooping sand for teeing up from the bottom of the hole!

Also there were evidently fewer and faster golfers who did not keep each other waiting by the quarter hour for every shot as is the hideous penalty we moderns have inflicted on ourselves in our so-called development of the game.

To cope with the larger number of regular local golfers, extra members of the R & A and the ever increasing loads of pilgrims to the shrine from all over the world, three more links have been constructed, the New Course in 1897 and the Eden in 1912. As their focal point, standing clear of the town buildings which flank the right-hand side of the eighteenth fairway, the massive stone clubhouse has a character all its own and is certainly imposing enough to the newcomer. Whether it was the stern countenance of the building itself or the prospect of the faces inside is debatable, but a new member of the R & A, attending the Autumn Medal for the first time in 1969, admitted

Lady Golfer, 1890.

84

to me that he spent more than twenty-four hours in the town before plucking up the courage to go in.

It is truly an unnerving moment, so much so that I personally had the temerity to suggest a system of reporting to the secretary with a view to being shown round and made to feel at home. I'm afraid, however, that we British are not much good at introductions and newcomers for years to come will continue to suffer agonies before settling into what is, after all, their own club!

It is an odd feeling also for the new-boy that some of the huge responsibility of the club devolves onto each individual in terms of having his say in all its traditional functions.

In conjunction with the United States Golf Association, the Rules of Golf are kept constantly under review, and though it constitutes no great tribute to those who draft the wordings the R & A even runs a decision service, answering queries which result from those odd happenings for which golf is famous, taking place as they do daily anywhere from Sunningdale to Tokyo to Augusta —but not, more's the pity, in Moscow.

What, for instance, is the right penalty or adjustment in strokes when the caddy of your opponent attends the flag, while you are putting, lifts the cup clear of the surface as he attempts to remove the flag and the ball is prevented from dropping by the rim? I cannot tell you, but the R & A can and does, thereby settling arguments which can so easily tend towards feuding between otherwise civilised folk. Incidentally, there is no game in the world which beginners happily play without first learning the rules, other than golf: truly an odd phenomenon.

Another important duty of the Club is to organise Championships and representative International Matches. On a national level the British Open, the Amateur, the Boys and Youths Championships are all run by the R & A; also teams for the Walker Cup, the World Amateur Team Championship and the Seniors Amateur Championship come under its aegis.

These are all in addition, I may say, to the actual members' Competitions which, with a widely held international membership, are also a rallying time for golfers from the world over.

There is this dual role within the club which makes some people understandably suspicious. Would it not be better, they say, to work on a more democratic basis, forming a separate governing body, made up of representatives from the golf unions of all the individual countries? Why should so much authority be vested in one obscure corner of the vast empire of golf? Why indeed? It is illogical to say the least. On the other hand, why not? There is no great advantage in rocking the boat while it is performing satisfactorily, and on the age-old basis of "better the devil you know" the R & A remains clear favourite to administer the game for as long as the members are prepared to do the job.

"THE GOLDEN BEAR"

THE biggest threat to Jack Nicklaus's career has always been, not the challenge of other golfers, but his own boredom with success.

Like Arnold Palmer, he counts achievement in terms of major titles and, having polished them all off within five years of turning professional, the second attempt at the "Slam" was not accompanied with quite the same resolve.

Wherever he plays, Nicklaus starts as favourite. He cannot be ignored. In nine years he won a million dollars prize money and was only the third man to do it. His reputation alone is enough to make him the short-price favourite no matter what the event.

He possesses a prodigious golfing talent which was recognised even when he was an amateur. When he decided to turn professional even the great Bobby Jones cabled him to re-consider because he felt Nicklaus was the only amateur who could repeat his feat—and beat the professionals in the major championships of the world.

But Nicklaus had made up his mind and in his first professional year was American Open champion. Inevitably he became a millionaire with a personal jet, homes in various parts of the United States and even an assortment of boats to cater for his obsessional past-time of fishing, both sea and lake variety.

When Nicklaus is in the mood, he cannot be beaten. He is one of the longest, and most accurate, hitters in the game and, at his best, can harness this power to a superb putting touch. But his problem has been—and will always be—to keep that talent on the boil. The pattern of his golf since that immense initial impact has been one of barren periods, spectacular eruption, then silence—until the next time.

When he came to St. Andrews for the British Open in 1970, three years without a major world title, he was acutely aware of the nakedness of his prestige. He felt it was time to win and ignored all distractions, including a

Nicklaus is possibly the best golfer in the world—his only problem is he sometimes get bored.

For such a big man, Jack Nicklaus has small hands and uses an interlocking grip to get more control of the club.

lucrative pro-amateur event, to plan his strategy for the Old Course.

Fate, it seemed, agreed it was his turn to win. After 72 holes he slumped in the clubhouse convinced he had thrown it away in the last few holes to the irrepressible short-swinging Doug Sanders. Yet, within 24 hours, Nicklaus was British Open champion.

By some monstrous stroke of misfortune which will haunt him for the rest of his life, Sanders missed his last putt to become champion. In the 18-hole play off the following day, he offered a blistering counter attack on Nicklaus whose peerless iron play had forced an early lead.

But Nicklaus would not let go. On the last tee, he removed his sweater, and lashed the ball 380 yards to the green for a birdie three and the title. As he boarded a transatlantic jet homewards, the priceless trophy in a wooden box tied with string, he observed: "To be remembered for all time, a man must win at St. Andrews." But even before that, Nicklaus was part of golf's history.

Nicklaus sinks a long one on his way to the first British Open title at Muirfield.

His flying right elbow, critics said, would undermine Nicklaus's consistency. But he has won every major title in the world and sees no reason for changing.

"THE TOY BULLDOG"

THE "Faithful Few" is a select group of men whose very existence is testimony to the axiom that nobody loves you when you're down, if not out. They are a handful of Brian Huggett's close friends who believed in him when he went through the worst patch of his career. At the time, he had all but been written off and his two tenacious finishes in the British Open were put down as inspired opportunism, nothing more.

The Faithful Few now meet once a year with righteous satisfaction. Their founder is now the most accomplished and competent of Britain's home-based professionals; a man whose status has risen internationally but who keeps the main area of his activity on the home circuit.

Huggett, son of a professional, was tagged "the toy bulldog" because he is small but grimly resolute. His preference for fast seaside courses was said, at one time, to be because he couldn't hit the ball very far and gained obvious assistance from a concrete-hard fairway. This may have been true, but the introduction of the larger 1.68-inch golf ball to British tournaments changed all that.

Huggett mastered the ball by lengthening his clubs to give him a wider swing and therefore more speed to hit the ball farther. When this combined with his basically sound putting technique, he was fully equipped to dominate.

The irony is that his bad patch started with his putting. He was always good on the greens, perhaps because of his need to compensate for a lack of length with the other clubs. But when this, the best part of his golf, suddenly wavered, he was in trouble. "Confidence starts to go with the putting," he said at the time. "You start wondering whether putts will drop—instead of knowing they will. You can't control it and it seems to spread right through your golf."

The Welshman concentrates so hard on a golf course that he can sometimes walk past his friends and relatives without noticing them.

The wide arc through the ball is what a small man like Huggett needs to get his distance.

"You've got to take the good with the bad!" Here's some of the bad—as Huggett misses.

But it would be unfair to dismiss Huggett's rise to the top of British golf as being simply the result of the change to the larger golf ball. The Welshman has matured into a wise performer, the man with a real chance in every tournament, who has a profound belief in his own destiny.

"For a long time I've been convinced that I am destined to win the British Open," he said. "I know I've been good enough to do it. When you've finished as close as I have to the winner, you know it's possible. I first knew it when I finished two strokes behind the champion. That's half-a-stroke a round. Not very much between me and the title."

Huggett, now thirty-four, has no desire to tackle the American professional circuit as Jacklin, Townsend and Barnes have done. In his earlier years, he toured the Far East winter circuit to gain experience. Now he confines himself to Europe and goes to the United States only as a matter of duty—either as an invitee to the U.S. Masters or as a member of the British Ryder Cup side.

"For one thing, I can't see any point in winning money abroad and then paying tax when I come home," he says. "Anyway, I like it here. Presumably the boys who go over there love that kind of life. But it's not for me."

GOLFING HAZARDS

Courtesy of PUNCH

"Before we married you conceded putts TWICE this long."

"Ah, Constable. Thank God! Back there in the copse by the second tee, woman with a knife in her back—looks in pretty bad shape."

THE GOLDEN PUTTER

WHEN a left-handed bank clerk won the New Zealand Open back in 1954, most people considered it one of those inexplicable flukes that sometimes happen in golf. The bank clerk, of course, had other ideas.

That was $250,000 ago. Bob Charles now realises he was absolutely correct to stop counting other people's money and begin accumulating some of his own through a formidable golf talent.

His initial impact was that of a freak. Nobody had reached world class tournament golf with a left-handed style. Even Ben Hogan, a natural left-hander, had decided to play the game in an orthodox manner. But Charles refused to turn round "the right way". Since his debut in professional golf, he has been British Open champion, Canadian Open champion, World Matchplay champion and a regular winner on the American professional tour.

He has shaken off his "freak" image and is now acknowledged to be one of the few international golfers who can strike form anywhere in the world.

He is probably the best putter in the world and the rest of his game has a steadiness aimed solely at getting him on the green without incident so that he can get to work with his incredible putting. He overwhelmed Phil Rodgers in the 1963 British Open play-off with phenomenal putting, and even though Gene Littler outplayed him in the World Matchplay final at Wentworth in 1969, the New Zealander was redeemed and eventually taken to victory by his devastating touch on the greens.

He says: "I reckon I can out-putt most of the other guys. I know if I can get the ball on the green I have a better chance than most of them. I really expect to hole everything within eight feet of the hole. Anything longer than that, is really a question of reading the greens correctly. But I don't get too upset if I miss them."

In that Matchplay 1969 final, he couldn't miss them. From 40 feet, he decided to "lag up" to the tenth hole, but the ball dropped. He faced a putt from 30 feet on the last hole to save the match and it dropped for him.

As sinister and deadly as a gunslinger—when he's on the course—stone-faced Bob Charles sees nothing funny about tournament golf.

The old repeating-swing is enough to get Bob Charles on the green and let his lethal putter get to work.

Below: Bob Charles goes for a dip in a bunker during '68 Alcan.

When Jack Nicklaus bore down on Charles to challenge him for the 1968 Canadian Open it was the New Zealander's putting that decided the issue. Nicklaus said afterwards: "Bob never made a mistake. He never hit a putt that didn't look as though it was going in. But that's Bob Charles. He putts consistently better than anyone else on the professional tour."

Charles says: "I learned pretty early on the American tour that every week there are fifty fellows good enough to win. They all have a good long game and they can all keep the ball in play. So it boils down to who can get the ball into the hole in the fewest putts. So you realise that it's only your putting that matters once you reach a certain standard and can stand up to the pressures.

"I don't think being left-handed presents any more problems when playing a course. That's why I would never tell a natural left-hander to try and play the so-called orthodox way. It hasn't done me any harm!"

THE KENTUCKY BUSINESSMAN

IF professional golf is stricly an entertainment industry then Frank Beard, from Kentucky, is in the wrong business. Beard is American golf's "Man in a Grey Flannel Suit". With him, it's strictly business. No glory, historical aspirations or drama. Just cash in the bank. And already, this business-like attitude has earned him over half a million dollars prize money.

He is thirty years old and, at this stage in his career, has no urge to establish himself as an international star golfer. His visits to Britain have been in the line of duty rather than personal ventures. His first two attempts at golf on the more natural and rugged type of British seaside course were not satisfactory. In the 1968 Alcan Golfer of the Year championship at Royal Birkdale, he failed to break 80 in two rounds. When asked what he thought of the course, he muttered: "I came to this country to make friends. Not enemies. I don't think I should say anything about it."

He tangled with Royal Birkdale again in the 1969 Ryder Cup and, in four matches, was successful only once. Even then he was partnered by Billy Casper.

Beard frowns upon the extrovert antics of other professionals and says: "Lee Trevino could do better if he didn't walk along joking with the galleries. And Chi Chi Rodriguez is another good example of what I mean.

97

First day nerves, as Frank Beard misses a short putt on the first day of the Ryder Cup.

"For me, tournament golf is like any other job. It's not drudgery, but it's not fun either. If you let it be fun, then 60 fellows taking it seriously will beat you every week. They'll smother you like a swarm of locusts."

But this disapproving attitude towards the light-hearted approach of others earned a sharp retort from the outspoken American professional Dave Hill: "If he doesn't enjoy the game, he ought to be doing something else. I know where he can get a job working in a petrol station."

Beard's golf technique is flawlessly simple, but his great asset is the ability to putt almost infallibly under pressure.

He won a tournament in 1963, his first professional year, then was taken seriously ill the following season and almost died. He was asked to accept the Ben Hogan Award for the golfer who makes the bravest comeback to the top, but he refused. His explanation: "I didn't do anything. I just got well again. There's no merit in that."

He is well on his way to his first million dollars and the point must come, as it has with most golfers of class, where money for its own sake means less than a desire to assess his own talent against world standards.

Left: Back on form, he holes an eagle putt.

THE TELEVISION PRODUCER'S NIGHTMARE

IF you fancy the quiet life, never tangle with anything that might involve trying to relate two such ill-suited entertainment mediums as golf and television.

They were never meant for each other. They would never, in normal circumstances, have got within touching distance, yet, under great pressure, the two have endured every stage of togetherness from the first exploratory cuddle, through years of stormy courtship until now they are firmly wed.

Arguments rage. Divorce is always on the cards but public demand manages to maintain them in their uneasy union.

The game of golf has literally none of the standard television ingredients.

There is very little action; it is slow moving; it takes an unconscionable time to arrive at a winner—loser situation and the critical moment in any match or tournament can occur at any point on a five-mile stretch of open country with no guarantee that the vital camera shot will, even then, be free from interference by a masking tree or passing spectators. What television programmer with his wits about him is ever going to be sold on that sort of deal if he has any choice in the matter?

The fact is simply that television has no choice. The public wants the big tournament action as and when it happens and if they are denied there is hell to pay.

The net result has been one of the costliest enterprises, in terms of technical production, that television has ever mounted. At a recent U.S. Masters' Tournament at Augusta no fewer than twenty-eight cameras were used and you can imagine what that means in terms of siting and building temporary structures, power lines, generators and overall co-ordination. By comparison, a standard outside broadcast unit has, at the most, five cameras, sufficient to give full coverage of a cricket Test Match or Wimbledon tennis.

Now take the problem of timing. There is really nothing to say how long the leading golfers will take to play.

People at home want to see the winning putt and how the champion played

100

the last few holes to secure his crown, and to guarantee them that service, live, is well nigh impossible.

What is there to stop someone from the pack playing a fantastic low round and being comfortably settled in the bar with a winning score before the television camera crews finish their tea-break let alone record him in action? Nothing. All they can do if that happens is show how all the leaders lost!

Spare a thought too for the commentators, especially in the early rounds of an Open Championship, trying to make it sound exciting when the appointed television time comes round and they are lumbered with a series of unknowns and has-beens to talk about.

I can hear Henry Longhurst's distinctive style now. "This is Joe Bloggs with a wedge, with just this little chip and a putt for a five which will put him, let's see, twenty-one over par. Oh dear! He lifted his head and that looks like costing him a seven. Well, we have all done it, etc., etc."

You are told not to expect to see your favourite, whether he be Coles or Crampton or Charles because he is still in the club house having lunch; which is where commentators would often dearly like to be at such soul-destroying moments.

I am talking mainly now of seventy-two-hole medal events, though match-play can be almost worse.

The highly successful Piccadilly Match Play tournament which has become such a fixture at Wentworth has had the luck of the devil in tele-vision terms, with important matches often going the distance when there is every possibility they will finish way out in the country with no chance of camera recording. Luck has been with them all the way until 1969, that is, when everything went wrong at the last moment.

Littler seemed to have done the right thing by the sponsors, the television production team and, of course, those sitting at home when he took Charles all the way to the eighteenth and then hit two glorious wood shots into the heart of the green. Meanwhile Charles was having trouble skirting the woods on the right and so the bed-time story looked like ending happily with a last-hole win for Littler—just before T.V. News-time.

Charles, unfortunately, was not party to the arrangement and proceeded to hole his fifteen-footer for a half.

Agonies of frustration resulted as the players set off down the first with no cameras in position while the viewers were left high and dry waiting for the result which, even when it came, seemed nothing but a dry statistic com-pared with the warm-blooded inside story of the live show they had been watching.

Actually I see no reason why television should not be accommodated by the golfers when it comes to extra holes. Tradition is the only obstacle, and in many ways it would be preferrable to have them playing the finishing hole or holes again, whether for television's sake or for the spectators who have worked hard for a last-green grandstand view.

Golf, like many other games, has already adapted in various ways itself to fit in with camera angles, light values, outside broadcast hours, programme schedules and all the rest of the complexities of broadcasting. Most significant of the various forms tried has been the matching of champions exclusively for recording purposes, every shot covered from two or three angles and the whole lot cut and edited down to the appropriate length. Shell's "Wonderful World of Golf" follows the same principle, each match taking a full day to shoot, even without taking muffed strokes over again, a refinement which, I am assured, has never happened yet.

"The Big Three" was one such series which ran a long while in the heyday of Player, Palmer and Nicklaus. For my taste it became too much of a good thing because once all the tricks of the trade were run through, the slow-motion shots and the semi-rehearsed spontaneous comments of the players, there was precious little left except perhaps the helicopter rides down the fairways: they had a sort of fairground appeal. But nobody could talk me into getting excited about which of the three actually won, mainly because three millionaires just don't get to squabbling over the difference between three thousand and five thousand dollars.

The series between the U.S.A. and the rest of the world was rather better. You could at least feel a little needle creeping in, but nothing like the real thing when the show is live and reputations are at stake.

Other potted versions have been tried. Target golf seemed to offer the easiest way through the time and distance tangle and enjoyed a short-lived popularity, but in the end it all comes back to television acting best in its only valid role, that of a live visual communication system covering newsworthy events. Television can get away, to an extent, with canned comedy shows and prepacked Westerns, but when it comes to golf, of all games, all attempts to use the medium other than live soon reveal themselves for the devices they really are.

So we leave our television friends to find the funds and the ways and means to bring us our ration of birdies on the box. We don't want to know about the spectator who has just poked his shooting stick through a power cable and we don't give a jot if the commentator, miles from the scanner, has lost all contact with the outside world and can only guess from his monitor what he is supposed to be describing.

We just want to see the best that golf has to offer. We pay for our licence and we know our rights.

Wentworth 1969 — Littler, right, and Charles produced problems for the camera.

103

WHAT MAKES TONY RUN?

Two weeks after Tony Jacklin learned that Peter Butler had bought a £5,000 Jensen car, he went out and bought himself a £7,000 version. There was no doubt in his mind which professional golfer in Britain should have the best car.

Jacklin has a compulsion to be Number One. It is his strength and perhaps that underlying force which took him to an Open championship no other British professional had won in eighteen years.

The signs of his magnificent conceit have always been there—from the time he drove that small red Ford and always blared the horn as he overtook. Those gold cashmere sweaters and matching silk trousers. Even the double-or-nothing bets when he couldn't cover the original stake. Somebody once kidded him in the early days about how much he, a minor professional, had charged a magazine which carried his picture. He smiled grimly and said: "One day, chum. One day."

In the early days opinions certainly divided on whether his confidence was founded on talent or narcissistic vanity. But there was a depth of character to this man which nobody, except those close to him, could recognise. Certainly there was a powerful ambition which he found difficult to hide. But he had punished himself with long hours of practice and weight-training in its pursuit.

Even before he had won a tournament in Britain, he admitted frankly: "I would be wasting my time if I didn't want to be the best golfer in the world. A lot of players in Britain are content to make a reasonable living playing reasonable golf. But that is not for me."

Something made him different, set him apart from the hundreds of other British professionals in this country. And it is too glib, and unfair, to suggest that two years on the virile American circuit turned him into a man or that those months away from home put the British Open into a different perspective—and made it just another tournament to win. Without doubt, Jacklin learned the American techniques and grasped the fundamental knack of being able to cope with pressure.

Dave Thomas, a shrewd judge of professional golf, said: "That last drive in the 1969 British Open surely made it obvious. He was as tight in his stomach as any man could be. But he could still keep his rhythm, still make a perfect pass at the ball when the tension was at its height. That's what he learned in America."

But even this must be a sophistication, a refinement, of some basic quality.

Jacklin learned the American secret—how to swing in a relaxed style when everything depends on it. He proved it in the 1969 British Open.

It is probably an absence of fear and consequent total disregard of failure.

As a youngster, Jacklin pipped the local newsagent by selling newspapers outside the gates of a Scunthorpe steel works. In 1967, he flew back from a tournament in Canada and, without sleep or practice, set about winning the British Assistants' title. That same fearlessness urged him into American golf when others cautioned him to consolidate his emerging success in Britain.

In the 1967 Ryder Cup at Houston, Texas, he was swamped in the singles by Arnold Palmer, and a powdered American matron in the crowd observed loudly: "Fancy putting a little boy like that against that big strong man!" A year later, he held off Palmer and the rest of the top American golfers to win the Jacksonville Open, the first British golfer to make impact since the frontier days of Vardon and company.

His technique was nothing special. It had a jerkiness and tendency to quickness which went with the temperament. But the constant American tournament grind taught him a magnificent control of this latent weakness which never showed when dramatically turning the tables on the Americans to win their Open championship at Hazeltine in 1970—but returned in the pestering winds of St. Andrews later that year as he sought vainly but gallantly to defend his title.

But his greatest gift is a majestic competitive arrogance, a refusal to be overwhelmed or dominated by any situation. He will attack at all costs. At one time, this urge to force the pace was thought to be his weakness. But Jacklin has always been aware that while a man might not be master of his own fate, he is entitled to give it a gentle nudge now and then.

One incident in that 1969 Open typifies all that is Tony Jacklin. It was a hole somewhere early on in the tournament and he had hooked into the willow scrub and the ball was lying deep. There was a high bank a few feet in front of him. It would have been standard recovery procedure to hack out and still have a chance of an iron and single putt for a birdie. But Jacklin was about to force it. He reached for a wood and even the hackers in the gallery knew his chances of success were little better than nil. The ball rocketed into the bank and ricocheted over. He had gained no more than forty feet. And the ball was under a bush.

At that moment, anybody would have accepted this was going to be an expensive hole. But Jacklin saw it differently. He hacked back to the fairway, flayed an iron 25 feet from the flagstick then brazenly ran down the putt for a par-five. That's what it showed on his score-card. Yet it hid the drama and essence of Jacklin.

He is an irrepressible young man and acutely aware of his responsibilities as a champion golfer. While he enjoys the limelight, he makes no attempt — nor needs — to hog it.

He comes from downright honest-to-goodness Lincolnshire stock. His father was a lorry driver and his delightful mum calls everybody "luv". And even though he is earning annually something in the order of £40,000 and is assured of £200,000 in business contracts over the next decade, he has no wish to forsake the place of his childhood. He has spent over £15,000 on a home there. And, while in big demand, he prefers the company of his local friends. He preferred, for example, to spend New Year's Eve at the office party of a Scunthorpe solicitor: "I used to work for him and he still considers me to be one of his staff. It's a marvellous feeling that not everybody regards you as an institution!"

What happened at Hazeltine in the American Open in 1970 was faithful to the Jacklinesque tradition. From somewhere in the lower reaches of the tournament field all season, he suddenly sprang into the lead in the first-round wind while others were blown into the eighties.

Was it impertinence to be there? Was it arrogance to think he could stay there? Three days later, he was American Open champion, and proved beyond doubt that what had been taken as splendid conceit was nothing more than the outward sign of a young man who knew the measure of his own talent and destiny.

With superb control, he kept the tempo of his swing slow at a moment when the pressures must have been compelling him to hit and hope. But in the last round, he started to drop strokes, and then was blessed with one of

The agony and the elation: First he missed a putt in 1969 Open when he knew he must keep ahead. But Jacklin persisted and walked from Royal Lytham's last green, his ball flung into the crowd. He was the first Englishman to win the title for 18 years.

those breaks of fortune every winner knows.

A long putt dropped on the ninth green. It jumped up in the hole then fell back. He confessed afterwards: "If that could happen, I knew then it must all be mine. It was a matter of playing one shot at a time. Of keeping my head clear and doing the best I could."

Historically, he became the first Briton in fifty years to take the American Open. Financially, he became the first Briton to become a golf millionaire. His income is now estimated at £200,000. Not bad for a young lad who only five years ago had to borrow a fiver to get home from the British Open.

"THE JOKER"

PAUL HAHN'S greatest trick has been to earn two million dollars from golf without ever winning a tournament.

He is an American professional golfer who realised quite early, in what looked like being an unsuccessful career, that his skill came in short bursts. He lacked the mental stamina to endure four rounds of tournament play. But he discovered a "ham" quality within himself. He could play to a crowd, not necessarily with brilliant golf; but even his near-misses provoked a response. From that flash of self-knowledge, he developed a repertoire of trick golf shots which made him a millionaire.

He travels 10,000 miles a year, mostly in his personal aircraft, putting on 200 shows all over the world. He even employs professional scriptwriters for the material to go with his act.

He sports an outrageous collection of clubs—a driver taller than himself ("I use it for playing over the fence of clubs that don't take visitors. Anyway my doctor told me to keep away from golf"). There's a hose-pipe with a club head attached; a club which is hinged to flop into three sections at the top of his backswing; even a miniature club—"It belongs to Mickey Rooney. He's so small he doesn't shout Fore. He says Two!"

"I'm really in showbusiness," Hahn says. "But it's an act based on golf. It takes me about six months to perfect a trick and I never try it until I'm absolutely sure. People still want to see skill even in a funny golf shot.

"But you're like a comedian. I've learned a lot from Bob Hope. He gave me one of my first scripts and he's advised me on technique. Sometimes it's probably tougher than tournament golf—you've got to make them laugh and play the shot right.

Every trick in the golf book. But Paul Hahn insists they need timing just like any other golf stroke. That, he says, is the secret of golf.

"I realise now I could never have withstood the pressure of tournament play. Well, I tried it—and I was broke. It was only when I missed a few putts that I realised that people reacted just as much as if the ball went in. I've got the trouper's approach. I've played to some pretty lousy audiences. Sometimes in pouring rain. I even did a show through an interpreter in Europe. It was terrible. Not one laugh. The crowd looked as miserable as a line of jock-straps. I don't know what this guy was telling them."

The high point of Hahn's act was his "William Tell Shot" in which he played a ball resting on a tee, held in the mouth of an assistant. Hahn had never missed but Ben Hogan warned him if he ever dipped on the shot, his career as a trick shot artist would be finished with one horrible accident. Hogan said: "You don't need it. Everybody misses a golf shot occasionally. Even me." Then Hahn heard there had been accidents involving youngsters trying to copy his trick so he dropped it from the act and has never used it since.

But there was still enough spectacular material in the act; like windmilling his way along two lines of golf balls, a club in each hand, and never missing.

He can produce a 250-yard drive, using either his giraffe driver, or the hose-pipe, the hinged club, or while standing one-legged on a stool—even seated. And he can hit a full drive from a waist-high tee. Then he does them all again, wearing a blindfold.

"The secret of my act is really the secret of golf," says Hahn who is now fifty and teaching his son the routine. "It's timing. Whatever the implement, the hose-pipe, long club, or broken one, the shot has to be timed properly to connect. It is the secret of strong and straight golf. Of course, the longer the shaft, the more I have to wait to connect.

"Before each season's tour I spend about eight weeks practising—but not the tricks. I just aim to perfect my timing with ordinary shots. I keep going until I feel that everything is co-ordinated. It's as though I'm fused into one unit. My mind and muscles are in tune—I can make my swing do exactly what I want. That's the only time I will try the tricks. After all, who wants to see tricks that aren't done right?"

CALIFORNIAN COWBOY

GEORGE ARCHER, the 1969 U.S. Masters champion, earned the nickname "cowboy" because he once worked on a ranch in California. Now, he owns one.

He is 6 ft 6 in, the tallest professional golfer in the world, with a curious habit of playing golf like a small man. He squats, as though sitting on an invisible chair, for all his strokes. And the advantage is that he eliminates the tall man's tendency to sway, yet still has a very wide swing to give the ball an extremely powerful blow.

He is also a success story in the old tradition. He was a caddy who so impressed a wealthy weekend golfer that he was sponsored. He worked on a ranch until he thought he was good enough to compete. His mornings were spent mending fences and the afternoons devoted to hitting golf balls in the fields.

The man who woke up in the night and pinched himself because he thought he dreamed he had won the American Masters. But it was true.

Archer's "sit-down" golf swing which keeps him steadier over the ball.

"I learned two things about tournament golf as a life," he says. "You've got to be the best. And you've got to enjoy what you do. The moment golf stops being fun, I shall quit. I enjoy the travel of the golf circuit. It's exciting and a rewarding way to make a living.

"What more could you want, besides a delightful family?" That, Archer also has. He named his two daughters after "the two most beautiful women in the world" — Elizabeth Taylor and Marilyn Monroe.

"I've developed a line of thought that everything is for the best," he says, "even though you don't know it at the time. Championships are important but I guess the top man in golf must be the one who earns most money. He's proved that, over the season, he is the best.

"I guess that's my goal, rather than winning all the championships which seems impossible for me to do. For instance, I couldn't believe I'd won the 1969 Masters. I woke up in the middle of the night and wondered whether it really happened. Somebody said at the time that the Masters would never be dominated again in the way the Big Three — Palmer, Nicklaus and Player — did it. There are too many good players around who can win.

"To me golf is a simple game. The technique is simple. People complicate it. I have the same technique I used as a kid. I tried to copy the top players and realised my own way was best for me. Perhaps now, somebody's trying to copy ME. But they'll learn!"

GRAHAM'S GOLF CLUB

THE CIRCUS

THE tournament golfer is part of a circus which plays to a different town each week. The customers and course may change. But the same old faces turn up on the first tee. His deep-rooted worry is that this week-to-week pilgrimage in pursuit of a low score and some cash will somehow blunt his performance into a tired habit. Each man is afraid he might lose his enthusiasm because somehow this is the key, perhaps the cause, of the sort of golf which earns big money.

Thus each performer develops his own philosophy to give some point to the gruelling pattern and to maintain the sharpness of his will to succeed. Inevitably, it will be assailed by setbacks.

Dave Thomas has been a tournament professional for almost twenty years and believes the "Oh-gosh-here-we-go-again" attitude is the most difficult problem a professional has to face. "There comes a point when nothing surprises you anymore," he said. "You accept, from your experience, that anything can happen. I suppose you become a fatalist. For a golfer, all experience can do— is punish you.

"You know you can spray one out of bounds on the last hole and lose. You've probably done it or seen it happen. Jacklin acknowledged the crowds as he walked on the last green during the 1969 Open. But he still hadn't holed out. I couldn't do that. And a lot of other pros couldn't. They know how disasters can suddenly grab you.

"The older pro envies the youngster's freshness. We try to get it—or retain

114

Dave Thomas is acknowledged one of the longest and straightest drivers in the world.

115

The best-looking golf swing in Britain belongs to Peter Alliss, son of a professional. Alliss says, "It's never been hard for me to swing a club. But putting—that's different."

"The Dependable" Bernard Hunt has a short back swing and steady short game which give him a reliability that always makes money.

116

it—by taking a few weeks off from the tournaments. It's one way of regaining your appetite for competition. I don't know one tournament pro who simply likes a game of golf. He thrives on the demands of competition."

Brian Huggett has made a deliberate and characteristically cautious progression to the top of British golf and he extols the virtues of patience. "You develop the philosophy that every week it's somebody's turn to win. It might be yours. But if not, there's always the next one. It's not a negative approach. But it stops you putting yourself under undue pressure and trying to win from the first tee. You play as best you can and then wait to see what happens. Maybe it will fall your way."

Peter Thomson, five times British Open Champion, is one of the best competitors in the world but even his philosophy has a touch of fatalism. "Winning a golf tournament is as much what other people do as what you do yourself. You can only get on with your own job and see if it's good enough."

George Will is a tournament professional of long experience and says: "You've got to learn how to play tournament golf. You learn the percentage game. It's not all death or glory. Rarely will you see a professional go for a shot if he has any doubt about how it will finish. Nobody fires at the flagstick if it's guarded by bunkers. They play for the middle and putt across. That way they get their par and perhaps a birdie. The other way, if it goes wrong, could mean a desperate struggle for par. Another trick is to try and set yourself up on any course for your best shots. I'm good with the mid-irons, so I try to tailor my game in a way that will leave me as many of these shots as I can get."

In such a small competitive community, the performers know each other's golfing likes and dislikes. A look at the course is enough to tell them who will do well that week. Most of them "chart" the tournament course in practice so that, whatever the wind conditions, they always know the distance to the green from where their drives land. They look for some landmark nearby and then pace its distance to the green.

"You see, it's our way of earning our money," says Thomas. "It's not glory, glory and cheers all the time. We're at business just like any businessman. I know a pro who sets his target at £100 a week. His whole game is geared to not doing anything silly enough to rob him of that money. He doesn't win very often—but he's got a nice big car."

"We're really playing at each other all the time," he adds. "For instance, if the wind's blowing a certain way we know Bernard Hunt won't like it. Or the greens might be slick enough to give Peter Alliss more than his share of problems. Everybody has their weak spots. And everybody knows them. I've never been able to chip well enough partly because I never needed it. I always had the power to reach any green. But if my accuracy starts to go—then I have to chip and I start using up too many strokes. But it's no secret. Ask anybody on the tour and they'll tell you my weak shot—just as I can do for anybody else."

This could be a joke, but Christy O'Connor doesn't regard golf as a laughing matter. A good scratch is something else.

It could be a raspberry Malcolm Gregson offers to his rivals. If so, it was deserved. He won the Tournament.

NOT WATCHING THE BIRDIE!

It missed — but only just. Max Faulkner once had 100 putters but he gave them all away: "It's the bloke using them — not the putter that matters!"

THE ORIGINAL DUBLINER

THE next big milestone in the life of Irishman Joe Carr ought to be his fiftieth birthday. But the Dubliner is undoubtedly more concerned about whether he can get back into Britain's Walker Cup side.

His Walker Cup service was unbroken for twenty-two years until, at the age of forty-eight, he narrowly failed to make the side which went to Milwaukee in 1969. It hurt him deeply and only hardened his resolve to qualify for the next side.

Carr is a legend in golf. From a humble background, he has become a very rich man with the biggest fashion business in Ireland and directorships of a bank and an insurance company. He was the second non-American to be invited to join the exclusive Augusta National Golf Club in Georgia (Sir Peter Allen, boss of ICI, was first).

Carr has been British champion three times and collected thirty other titles during his distinguished career. That ought to be enough for one lifetime. But Carr still wants to play golf—the best kind of golf. His life revolves around the desire to remain among the best amateurs in the British Isles. Even an ordinary working day begins with golf. At dawn, he runs three miles along the coast beside his home, then hits 100 practice shots.

He says: "It does my golf good. And even if it didn't, it must help an old fellow like me to keep in trim. Mind you, I'll probably have a heart attack on the beach one day—but why worry about it?"

Why does he carry on? He was playing Walker Cup golf before some of his current rivals were born. Legendary American amateurs like Billy Joe Patton and Charlie Coe came into the game after him, and have long since departed into history.

While Joe Carr can swing like this, there's no reason in the world for him to quit.

121

"I've been doing it for so long," says Carr, "I wouldn't know how to live without competitive golf. But I shall have to change my outlook. I thought recently that it's pointless a man of my age trying to hit his drives 300 yards. But if I'm shorter off the tee, that means my long irons have got to be better. Still, I might last a bit longer in the game if I made the change.

"I've been able to carry on this long because my competitive nerve lasted. This is what really ruins top players. The swing is the same, the shots are still there, but their nerve fails. It shows in the putting. But the big problem for me has been to retain my concentration. It's very difficult after all these years to keep thinking on one subject for eighteen holes. But all those years have their compensations.

"I've talked to Dai Rees and Sam Snead about it. There's nothing new to us. No situation or shot is ever new. We get more wise and less flustered. You'll never see an older man make an error of judgement. I feel now that if I can't get back into the team then at least I'll be a worthwhile obstacle for youngsters trying to make it.

"I try not to think about giving it up. I keep telling myself I'll have just two more years. But I've been saying that for a long time. Golf, at the top level, is part of my life. I don't know how I shall get on without it. Mind you, being Joe Carr counts for something. The reputation gives me a psychological advantage over an opponent—even if the golf doesn't!"

"Hey, Charlie—it's over here in the trifle."

"Number 3 or Number 4 iron, Mr. Perkins?"

GOLFING GAMBLERS ANONYMOUS

GAMBLING at golf is a creeping sickness which must be discouraged and stamped out where possible. This is the stated opinion of the Royal and Ancient Golf Club, St. Andrews, with particular reference to the type of competition known as the Auction Sweep. They fear the consequences when large sums of money are bid with the attendant temptation for the needy and greedy to work rather harder than they should to scoop the pool.

It needs no imaginative genius to work out how to go about winning an auction of this kind, though, like the professional backer of horses, it is not so much being certain of backing the winner as getting value for money when you do.

In golf, probably more than any other game, there are no certainties. What odds would you have laid, I wonder, against Gary Player beating Tony Lema when he was seven down with eleven to play round the Burmah Road at Wentworth? Ten to one? More like a hundred to one probably, and yet the impossible happened.

So, even if you manage to organise yourself an unfair handicap advantage in an Auction Sweep, there is no point in going for broke at the auction.

How are you to know that someone else is not playing the same game? And you cannot be sure that your secret weapon—let's say a one-time lady county champion, who gave up golf to have a family, and has now taken it up again with a handicap of twelve—has not been observed in training by the touts! You will soon know that the cat is out of the bag when the bidding goes high against you and then, like the backer of horses or the poker player, you must know when to cry "enough" and cut your losses.

There are so many slips between cup and lip in this kind of "swindle" that the fears of the R & A are probably groundless. Yet they have a stewarding job to do, much like the Gaming Board in relation to casinos, and they must draw the line somewhere. Personally I have always been more alarmed at the availability of fixed odds against a match like the final of the Piccadilly Match Play championship. All sorts of appalling possibilities present themselves

123

"A Lie." By Hassell.

MANSELL

from doping, to physical wobbling, all the way down to that most degrading moment which horse racing and professional boxing endures, when the public start to think that a match has been purposely thrown for profit.

Even though nine times out of ten suspicion of a jockey or boxer is entirely groundless, demonstrations against performers, umpires, stewards and referees constitute such an ugly blot on the sports where they happen that the less golf becomes involved the better.

Nevertheless, it is all a matter of degree. Some good judges are unflinching in their opinion that golf should be played solely for the pleasure which comes with winning. They even frown on a few shillings changing hands at the end of a Sunday four-ball and I have heard them forecast gloomily the gradual run-down of any club which gains a reputation for betting high.

On the other hand there are those who fully admit they get no kick out of the game unless they play for something they would prefer to win rather than lose. So I draw the conclusion that it takes all sorts to make a world and that people should be allowed to make their own rules so long as they are not downright wicked.

There have been crooks and cheats, mind you; doubtless far more than ever get found out. Some dubious goings-on can never be proved. Like the suspected dropping of an identical ball when the real one is found later. There is strong circumstantial evidence but nothing really to prove which ball was which.

Occasionally, though, some unfortunate gets caught red-handed. There was a case when a poor fellow hooked a ball wide into the woods at a slightly blind short hole after his opponent had apparently played a good one. Both players and their caddies then dived straight into the trees to look. Suddenly there was a shout that the ball had been found in a convenient clearing and it was duly pitched up to the pin.

Everyone now walked onto the green for the first time to find three balls sitting there, two with the same markings. Let it be a lesson to all those who get tempted, to make sure that the first one is well and truly lost!

For those who fancy an honest gamble on the golf course it is as well to know the tricks of the trade.

They should know the meaning of terms like corners, Nassau, Las Vegas, automatic presses and represses. Nassau, normally the generic name for three separate matches, on first nine, second nine and match, can have different variations depending on local custom.

It may give the first nine loser the option to double the stake on the back nine, and an inadvertent hiccup on the tenth tee may be taken as the signal that he wants a bet which he knows nothing about.

If you are not familiar with the system of "pressing", you should also step warily. There is no magic in the principle. It simply means that whenever either party stands two down in any match they can offer to play the remaining holes, starting level again, for an agreed amount. This is usually half the original unit but occasionally a full unit press is the standard practice, and it is as well to be sure which is intended.

The whole idea is to maintain a financial interest right up to the last hole where there is often a swing of many units resting on the final putt. Obviously it militates against the longer handicap man who seldom receives a stroke at the last hole, but the whole question of playing percentages is also raised and the shrewd gambler will hold his fire if the opportunity to "press" happens when he, for the sake of argument, has already received seven of his nine shots, and stands to get only two in the last five holes. The odds are against him.

One golden rule is to remain calm when someone starts offering you apparently many more than your quota of strokes according to handicap. There is bound to be a catch in it somewhere.

The conversation, probably after a drink or two, will go something like this: "I don't mind playing you," says the professional hustler. "What's your handicap?" "Twelve," you answer cautiously. "Well, I'll tell you what I'll do," says your earnest friend making out he's doing you a favour. "I'll give you a stroke a hole." Consternation. Surely only complete duffers need a stroke a hole. At this point the unwary rabbit's pride is stung. He has been shooting in the low eighties and sees no reason why he won't do so again.

"I'll play you for anything you like," the subversive voice goes on, and before you know where you are you have agreed a match off the back tees for fifty times more money than you have ever gambled before.

Your opponent has been through it all before and taking the honour at the first hole, as is his right, hammers one down the middle. Suddenly the match seems less easy to win as with shaking knees you take five at the first par four and lose it to a birdie. You are now one down for a month's salary and oh! how you wish you were back in your office earning it; instead of putting so much at risk in a game which you only play for fun.

When you eventually lose heroically on the seventeenth green and pay by cheque, the victor will swear he was a fool ever to make the bet. He had no idea you could play so well and would not fancy his chances in a return match. No Sir! It was only that bit of luck when his chip hit the stick at the sixteenth which stopped him from losing.

Be a man, my friend, and admit it when you are licked. Never play that seductive return match, even if you are offered a two-up start.

Like the gentleman said, "If he bets you he can make ink come out of his ear, you can rest assured he can make ink come out of his ear."

Admittedly you would have to fall into pretty low company to get taken for a complete ride but, if away on holiday somewhere, it is as well to be sure you are not the odd man out in a four-ball.

In this particular form of skulduggery you find yourself teamed up with not only the best player but also the man who apparently has all the money. He keeps "pressing" and increasing the bets despite playing unaccountably badly, includes you in on the deal, and promptly pays up with a smile.

What you must be quite sure about is that you are not playing one against three with your contribution being split three ways. Not a common connivance perhaps, but you can be sure it has been worked before now.

Gambling, wherever you find it, can act like a habit-forming narcotic on some people, and golfers are by no means immune. They rush compulsively to the course every weekend as though in a hurry to prove that their nerve will be better today than it was yesterday. I have seen quite good golfers deteriorate under the strain of continually losing, even though they can well afford the money, until no amount of extra strokes helps to right the balance.

I know brilliant golfers who have lost their edge altogether because they only need to keep the ball in play to collect the cash. They lose the art of attacking the pin, never take a risk and finally their genius deserts them. There is a need here not so much for the R & A but for a GGA — Golfing Gamblers Anonymous.

Yes, these are some of the less attractive sides to gambling at golf, but it is still hard to condemn those who enjoy it and who play within their means. You cannot draw the line simply by the size of the bet. There are those who punt far more heavily on bridge and backgammon to whom a hundred pounds on a golf match just means an inexpensive way of taking exercise and keeping fit for the real business in the evening, and those same people will usually get much more thrill out of their small interest in a golf game than from a whopping wager on a horse. Who is to deny them their bit of sport?

Everything is after all relative and if the R & A or anyone else is looking for a guide line in the matter, the old saying about "all things in moderation" seems to fit the bill.

THE MELBOURNE TIGER

THERE is enough ambition left within Peter Thomson to urge him beyond Harry Vardon's record of six victories in the British Open. But the Australian has other things to do first. His personal aim was pushed aside in recent years while he attempted a grand design for world golf. The object was to produce a global circuit almost equal in prize money to the United States tour.

Already, he has played a major part in establishing the Far East segment of the tour and he sees existing circuits, like Britain, South Africa, Australia and New Zealand falling into a sequence which will offer continuous tournament golf for player and spectator.

"In the Far East, I used myself as bait," Thomson, now in his forties, explained. "I promised to bring other professionals if various countries put up the money. It's good for the game and also gives an opportunity for talented players in those countries to earn a living from golf."

One of Thomson's primary objects in establishing this tour is to restore the balance in international golf and dissuade younger professionals from flocking to the American professional tour. The idea has special point in Britain where the best young players are already following the example of Jacklin and Townsend and, in so doing, depleting the market value of the home tour to possible sponsors.

The size of the American circuit presents a threat throughout the world not simply because of the six million dollars prize money on offer but because of the high standard of play. This is the key attraction for a young player who wants to improve.

Thomson has never been over-fond of American golf, or more generally, the American way of life. He is a placid, withdrawn man who prefers his own company. Not surprisingly, he found himself at odds in an extrovert society like the American tour. His reluctance to play there has been construed as an inability to master the larger 1.68-inch American golf ball—which he admits he doesn't like—as well as their courses. But his motives for a world circuit are not based on these old prejudices.

"Thank you very much, Ladies and Gentlemen. And for my next trick . . ." Peter Thomson gets the closest he can to emotion on a putting green.

His scheme is for a tour from Australia and New Zealand, through the Far East to India, then Africa and on to Europe and the British Isles. Already he has been promised a £50,000 award for the golfer who finishes in top position over this world season. He says: "Of course, the circuit would not be quite as wealthy as the American version, but a man could still become rich without going to the United States."

129

One of the great theorists in golf, Thomson believes that a good address position guards against most faults in a golf swing.

130

British golf has attempted to compensate for a lack of star material with all manner of novelty tournaments, but Thomson does not see this as the answer and adds: "Golf is stagnating in Britain at a time when it's booming in every other country." (It can be argued that even though tournament prize money has now reached £350,000, there is no long-term promise that this money will remain as in the case of the American and other circuits. The big sponsors are still not prepared to commit themselves.)

The Thomson Plan would bring a new breed of tournament golfer to Britain, top players from all over the world who were part of the world tour. But there are radical adjustments to be made to the British system. Thomson sees the British season being confined to major tournaments in a 12-week period spaced around the Open championship.

All these tournaments should offer a minimum £10,000 and be open to anybody who wants to play. Any sponsor who refuses these conditions should not be turned away but diverted to an off-peak period outside the 12-week run. This would mean that such a sponsor would get only those "Local" players not following the world tour because the main party, the big attractions, would be elsewhere.

"For a long time the world has been crying out for such a circuit," says Thomson. "The American tour is absolutely saturated and overflowing with people." Thomson admits that his own golf suffered with the preoccupation of his world dream. But he can foresee a point when he will be able to concentrate on personal ambition again.

"I still have the same urge to play," he says, "but my head is always full of other things. Once the world circuit is set up and going, perhaps I can turn my back on the politics of it and get back to playing." But in Britain, that means using the larger 1.68-inch ball which is compulsory in tournament play. Thomson, undoubtedly the best exponent of golf with the small 1.62-inch ball, is highly critical of this move which was based on the logic that the Americans use the bigger ball and they are better than us.

The theory behind the larger ball plan also accepted that it was more difficult to control because of its size. Those who mastered it must, it was concluded, be better golfers for this reason.

Thomson argues against its efficiency on the more natural British courses: "It certainly hasn't produced any better play. Tournaments have not been won with good hitting but by a good short game and good recoveries. This is the strength of American golf. If you play with the big ball, you learn its limitations. So you just try to keep it out of trouble. But it means you cannot achieve the accuracy or the low scores."

As Thomson says, there's always SOMETHING going on in his head. Like the vulnerability of Vardon's record. They allow the small ball in the British Open which is all the Australian ever needs.

131

THE WINNERS

THE game is littered with men who were good enough to win but never did. They lacked that indefinable quality of a winner. And a man never knows the truth about himself until he is confronted with his chance.

How he handles himself over those last few agonising holes, when every pressure bears down upon him and only his faith in himself can help, is the true test of whether he will ever be more than just a member of the supporting cast. Each man reacts differently, partly because of the situation. But all have endured the fear that precedes the most important moment of their careers—the point at which they broke away from the pack.

Jacksonville 1968 was the moment Tony Jacklin stepped into world class. The best players in the world were close on his heels as he faced the last round, sustained by a paltry one-stroke lead. "I had all the morning to kill before I teed off but I didn't want to get to the course too early and hang around. I went sight-seeing with a friend. Anything to keep my mind off the golf. I knew I couldn't play it safe. There were too many good players around. Palmer was playing with me and only one stroke behind. I went for everything because with people like Palmer breathing down your neck, you never know when they're going to fire a couple of birdies.

"After the seventeenth, I was three strokes clear. I was on my own. I stood on the last tee and desperately wanted to play the ball with a wedge all that way up the last hole—just to keep it out of trouble. But I knew that was no way to win.

"All the way round Palmer never said a word to me. He just looked now and again. I can never tell what he's thinking. But he was there to win. I played the last hole pretty badly but, as I was doing it, I knew nobody could catch me.

"I was bunkered round the last green. I didn't want to throw it away with a stupid bunker shot. I didn't care what the crowd thought, I took a putter to get the ball out because the trap was shallow enough. It cost me a six but I knew I was clear. And Palmer came over to shake my hand. I felt numb—as though it wasn't really happening."

132

A cautious drive — the big danger when a man is close to winning. He tried to play safe and protect his lead.

Oosterhuis is the boy who thought he was never going to win. Then he learned not to worry about it — and won!

Palmer: He's never afraid to attack, no matter what the danger.

The harrowing aspect of golf is that it gives a man, as he walks, time to ponder on all the things that might go wrong. Tommy Horton was on the threshold of winning the biggest championship of his life, the South African Open, when a thought occurred to him: "I suddenly remembered what Peter Butler told me about being in the lead. You drop a couple of strokes in the last round and you're devastated. You feel you've thrown it away. You're back in the pack.

"I was nervous as we started that last round. There were too many good players around me. In that situation, your professionalism takes over. All you've ever learned in tournament play suddenly becomes reflex.

"It's the reason we travel the world instead of just practising at home. You must get under the stress of competition, you must become nervous, just to learn how to control yourself under pressure. Then, one day, it's needed and you find out whether you're hard enough.

"I kept telling myself just to swing at the ball and keep it in play. I kept all thought of actually winning out of my mind. There was nothing I could do if somebody was going mad out there on the course. But I convinced myself they had to shoot a good score to get past me. And I was right. They didn't."

The sweet moment of success — the passport to a fortune — call it what you like, it is every tournament professional's dream. For, with the honour and the cash, can come an empire of businesses from clothing to dry cleaning stores.

The wives, like Barbara Nicklaus, share the pain of failure. They know what sweet success can be to their men.

Peter Oosterhuis, who turned from top amateur golf to the professional game, faced an acute and demoralising problem. Several times he had been clear enough to win, but had thrown the whole thing away with a series of last-minute errors. He began to suspect he could never win. Then, pursued by Gary Player, he took a five-stroke lead in the last round of the Western Province Open in South Africa.

"I had built up a good lead," he recalled. "My job was to hold on to it. But the big danger was Gary Player who was my partner. He could catch fire any time. I suddenly played on hole badly and thought "Oh God, I'm going to throw it away again." But Gary made a mistake and somehow my error didn't seem so disastrous.

"He didn't say anything to me all the way round. He is the complete competitor, trying to win every time he plays. He didn't encourage me and he didn't impede me.

"The last hole was a short one and when Player missed the green I knew it was all over. The crowd cheered my shot so I knew it was close. I didn't dwell over the shot as I stood there. I just went through the normal routine and hit it. It doesn't help to think just how important the shot could be. But once you've won, you know you can do it again."

But Bernard Gallacher's first professional triumph proved nothing. The young Scot had finished his round when Guy Wolstenholme, who had dominated the Schweppes tournament, suddenly bungled the last two holes and Gallacher found himself the winner. Later, when Gallacher had a fight on his hands against Brian Huggett for the Daks title at Wentworth, he chose the wrong strategy.

"I thought I had to play fantastic golf over the last few holes to win," he said later. "I'd been in the lead and lost it. I tried to finish with three birdies and it was a stupid plan.

"When the pressure is on, par golf is often good enough to win when time is running out. That's what I told myself later in the Wills tournament. I was one stroke behind Brian Huggett with six holes left. I told myself to forget about birdies and just try for level par. It eased the pressure and in fact I finished two under par. I didn't try and force the chances, but if they came I snapped them up."

Brian Barnes, in winning the Agfacolor, conquered more than his fellow

Player — the moment of triumph means he can ease the tension. Sometimes he cries and most times his wife Vivienne is there to console him.

Palmer — the old routine — another item for his trophy room — but will they get more scarce?

135

competitors. Until then, he had always been talented enough, but somehow never quite capable. He had an impulsive, and crucial uneven temperament.

"I had to believe I could win. Not just hope. That's never good enough. So before the tournament I read a book about positive thinking. In the last resort, it's your self-possession that carries you through. In the last round, on every tee, I said a prayer that this would be my day. Corny perhaps, but it kept me calm." He showed just how calm on the sixteenth, a short hole he had not hit all week. He was forced to stand around while the stewards forced back the crowd. It was the moment the old Barnes would have blown. This time, his long iron found the heart of the green. Barnes had learned how to win.

One of the strongest hitters in British golf, Brian Barnes, son-in-law of Max Faulkner, is reckoned by American critics as a definite candidate for success on their circuit.

THE OLD FIRM

IT is quite safe to assume that men like Neil Coles, Peter Alliss, Bernard Hunt and Christy O'Connor will always find themselves near the top in any tournament list. Yet the monotony of their appearance there, somehow belies the talent they muster to stay on top. It overlooks the enormous scope of professionalism that means they can deliver the goods week after week.

They are, in fact, The Old Firm. But, in the ever-expanding world of golf, they have assumed a new, possibly unique, importance. They could be the last of the line in professional golfers who have taken the sport on their own terms.

Because of this, they have never quite reached the promised peak. But it would be wrong to undervalue their skill. Most are world class.

As Dave Thomas says: "Does being a professional golfer mean you can't be a good father to your kids? I love just to take them to school and natter with other parents. I like to go and see my local football team play. Why must you miss out on these things?"

Thomas came close twice to being British Open champion—once he got to a play-off with Peter Thomson at Royal Lytham and another time just failed to catch Jack Nicklaus at Muirfield. Thomas was so impressive that Gary Player offered to sponsor him on the American tour. But the Welshman, after only a few months, got homesick then hurt his back, and came home. He has never gone back as a serious contender.

Neil Coles is acknowledged to be one of the best golfers in the world. Certainly he ranks in the top fifty. But he hates to fly and this phobia has cost him thousands of pounds. It began several years ago as an attack of claustrophobia in an aeroplane and now he cannot force himself to travel by air. In 1967 he insisted on taking a boat trip to the Houston Ryder Cup while the rest of the British team flew. For tournaments in Ireland, he undertakes an arduous car journey then overnight boat ride. But Coles thinks it is worth the effort.

He could not endure the rigours of the American professional tour where taking an aeroplane is as natural as taking a practice swing. Even his immensely successful European run—when he earned £5,000 in just over a month—was done by car.

Deeper psychological motives lay at the root of Peter Alliss's failure to transfer into success one of the best golf swings in the world. A phrenologist once said he lacked concentration. Some people have suggested that he has an over-awareness of his famous golfing father. Alliss himself admits that the prowess of hitting a golf ball has never presented any problems to him.

But he is an imaginative and sensitive man. And imagination, unchecked, is a golfer's greatest enemy. Alliss, too, may be developing a little disenchantment with the performing aspect of professional golf—and is now well established as a golf course architect, writer and television commentator and he shows beginnings of a script-writing talent. Brilliant in man-to-man match-play, he seems unable to maintain the same personal pressure against the more abstract enemy of medal play.

Bernard Hunt, it is said, once aimed to make £100 a week from professional tournaments and winning if it came, was a bonus. But his basic concern was to produce a money-making swing—simple and faultless. He has one of the shortest backswings in golf and is one of the most consistent performers.

Christy O'Connor is the man everybody likes to watch. He plays the way everybody else would like to—with a languid, fluid and full swing plus a no-nonsense putting method. When it all jells, generally before his native Irish crowd, Christy is unbeatable. He has never offered that same aggression on foreign soil. Yet the living is good when you're Christy O'Connor, "king" of Dublin.

Christy O'Connor driving off from the tee.   *Close-up of Neil Coles.*

DAYTON, OHIO

DAYTON, Ohio, has the sad historical distinction of being the place where a golf tournament was first used as a platform for demonstrators.

Their arguments may have been valid. They wanted some say in how $200,000 profit from the American PGA championship was to be distributed among the poor. But they did not win their case.

Their tactics, however, had a devastating effect. It took two hours to ruin the chances of Gary Player and Jack Nicklaus. It needed only a cup of ice, a shout, a souvenir programme and a handful of hotheads to achieve maximum impact.

Ed Carter, the tournament organiser, knew the assault was planned. There were 400 police and security men waiting for the first signs. Somewhere among 23,000 people, trouble would break out. It could not be prevented, but it could be stamped on quickly. The crisis point would arrive on Saturday afternoon when the championship went on nationwide television.

Gary Player and Jack Nicklaus, paired together, turned out to be the targets. They were star material, both in contention for the lead and an obvious attraction for the television cameras. Thus would the demonstrators make coast-to-coast protest. They warmed up in the wings. On the fourth tee, out of camera shot, somebody hurled a programme at Player as he addressed his ball. Nicklaus got a laugh by pretending to hide behind his golf bag.

On the ninth green, as Nicklaus crouched over a birdie putt, the stillness was shattered by a man's shout. Nicklaus stepped away, smiled, and missed. The rehearsal was over.

As Player picked his way through the crowd in front of the clubhouse towards the tenth tee, somebody shouted his name. He turned and received a cupful of ice in the face.

"What have I ever done to you?" he asked.

"You're a damn racist!" was the answer.

It was a bearded man and before he could argue further, the Pinkerton Squad had grabbed him and led him away. Player was clearly shaken and Nicklaus said afterwards that suddenly he thought of his wife and son who were watching it all somewhere in the crowd.

Neither man could know, as they walked towards the tenth green, that this was to be the arena chosen by the demonstrators. A negro broke from the crowd and charged, head down, at Nicklaus.

The golfer drew back his putter — "I didn't want to hit him. I kept hoping he'd stop before I had to. I wondered where my wife and son were."

Some instinct made the negro change course and he may well have reflected in Dayton jail that night how wise he had been not to test the full fury of perhaps the strongest golfer in the world.

But the demonstrator's act was the signal for a gang to break loose. Nicklaus's ball, waiting for a possible eagle three, was thrown away. Player's golf ball, near enough for a birdie, suffered similarly.

Even so there was a flash of nightmarish humour as one demonstrator charged towards Player and said he wanted to speak.

"This has got nothing to do with your being South African!"

"Is that supposed to make me feel better about it?"

The police moved quickly and the demonstrators were carried off. Nicklaus replaced his ball but missed the eagle. Player's downhill putt, difficult enough without the prelude of a mass arrest, curled smartly into the cup to a delighted roar from the crowd. It was the end of the trouble. But neither man knew it.

Police refused to allow them the short walk through the crowd to the press tent. Instead, they were taken under armed guard to a basement in the clubhouse for their press conference.

Nicklaus looked dejected: "Count me out of this championship. I don't want to give these people the credit of attention by even talking about them. But I was scared out there. Will we have guards tomorrow?"

Player drew a smile: "It was like a game of 'gotchas'. I stood over the ball and thought who's going to grab me next? I can't play that way. I'm not looking forward to going out there tomorrow."

The contenders went out under police escort the next day. But Player and Raymond Floyd, the leader, had a special guard. Every green was ringed by this personal bodyguard who faced the crowd waiting for trouble.

But the only drama that day was to be the golf. Eleven demonstrators had been arrested the day before and their assault was over, although nobody knew

140

Piccadilly '66. Nicklaus on safari at the 13th hole of the Burma Road (as the West Course at Wentworth is called) during the Final.

Definitely not a hole-in-one — but Gary Player is almost as delighted. At least he's clear of that terrible rough.

it at the time. Player started to revive his interest as Floyd, nearing his first major title, showed nervous tension by visiting the woods in pursuit of his golf ball. But the American stayed just beyond the reach of Player who lost by a single stroke.

Player met Nicklaus afterwards in the clubhouse and asked if there had been any trouble with demonstrators. Nicklaus grimaced: "The hell with demonstrators. This big cop bothered me. He looks at one hole and says he doesn't like the look of the crowd on the left of the green. Could I knock the ball over to the right?"